Hispanic American Achievers
High-Interest Nonfiction

by Kathryn Wheeler

Carson-Dellosa Publishing Company, Inc. · Greensboro, North Carolina

CREDITS

Editor: Carrie Fox

Layout Design: Lori Jackson

Inside Illustrations: Nick Greenwood

Cover Design: Peggy Jackson and Nick Greenwood

Cover Illustration: Tara Tavonatti

This book has been correlated to state, national, and Canadian provincial standards. Visit *www.carsondellosa.com* to search for and view its correlations to your standards.

ISBN 978-1-60022-968-8

Table of Contents

Introduction

Invite your students to experience the thrill of reading with the historical biographies in *Hispanic American Achievers: High-Interest Nonfiction*.

The passages in this book are appropriate for students in the intermediate grades. Among these grade levels, you will find learners at all different reading levels. When presenting students with a new text, there is always the danger of either frustrating struggling readers or boring those students who have jumped ahead. To help all of these students maintain interest and find success in their reading assignments, this book presents each passage at two reading levels.

Also included with each passage are a set of comprehension questions that applies to both versions of the story and a bonus activity. The questions test students' skills in determining main ideas, using context clues, sequencing, reading for details, and drawing conclusions. The assessment grid at the back of the book makes it easy to see which reading comprehension skills each student has mastered.

Each bonus activity is a writing extension that reinforces reasoning skills and encourages students to connect prior knowledge with the text.

An icon in the lower right or left corner of each passage designates the reading level.

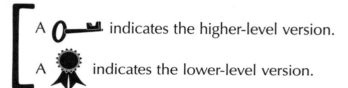

A ⌐—◖ indicates the higher-level version.

A ✸ indicates the lower-level version.

Use the rubric below to help you assess students' writing after they complete the bonus writing extension following each passage.

	Novice	**Emerging**	**Independent**	**Distinguished**
Topic	Did not stay on topic	Stayed on topic for most of the paragraph	Stayed on topic	Stayed on topic with elaboration
Organization	Not organized	Organized	Well organized	Outstanding organization
Written Expression	Hard to understand	Easier to understand	Easy to understand	Well written, elaborated

Father Junípero Serra
(1713–1784)

Junípero Serra was born on an island called Majorca, a part of Spain. As a child, he was an excellent student. He became a priest after his 15th birthday and was given a job as a teacher at a university when he was 24. He taught religion.

He had a quiet life. It allowed Father Serra to use his mind. It protected his poor health. But, Father Serra had a different idea of what his life should be.

In 1749, Father Serra asked church officials if he could travel across the ocean. He wanted to go to Mexico City, Mexico, because priests there were setting up a mission, and he wanted to help. His ship landed in Vera Cruz. Father Serra insisted that he could walk to Mexico City. The small, **frail** man walked more than 200 miles to get there, amazing those who traveled with him.

Father Serra worked in Mexico for 15 years. Then, his life changed again. In California, there were several missions. Father Serra was put in charge of them. The priest, who had asthma and a leg injury, made the long trip to California. The next year, Spain wanted to make sure that it kept a strong hold on the northern part of California. Father Serra was asked to set up even more missions. This would help Spain keep a close watch on its territory in western North America.

Father Serra spent the rest of his life walking and riding across California. Many areas had never been explored. He set up nine missions across 700 miles of land. He sent back reports about what he saw and found in the new country. In some places, the roads were rough and rocky. It made riding difficult. In other places, he found cool streams, riverbanks

covered with roses, and grapes growing wild. He met many American Indians. He said that they all treated him well.

In 1784, Father Serra was 70 years old. He had traveled back and forth across California many times, traveling an estimated 24,000 miles. This hard life of camping, walking, and riding was difficult for him. He died at one of his missions. But, he had opened up new land. Thanks to this explorer, much of early California was settled.

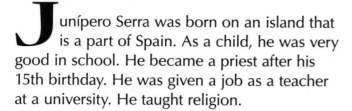

Junípero Serra was born on an island that is a part of Spain. As a child, he was very good in school. He became a priest after his 15th birthday. He was given a job as a teacher at a university. He taught religion.

He had a quiet life. It let Father Serra use his mind. It guarded his poor health. But, Father Serra had a different idea of what his life should be.

In 1749, Father Serra asked church officials if he could travel across the sea. He wanted to go to Mexico City, Mexico. Priests there were setting up a mission. He wanted to help. His ship landed in Vera Cruz. Father Serra said that he could walk to Mexico City. The small, **frail** man walked more than 200 miles to get there. The people who went with him were amazed.

Father Serra worked in Mexico for 15 years. Then, his life changed again. In California, there were several missions. Father Serra was put in charge of them. The priest had asthma and a hurt leg. But, he made the long trip to California. The next year, Spain wanted to make sure that it kept a strong hold on the northern part of California. Father Serra was asked to set up more missions. This would help Spain keep a watch on its land in western North America.

Father Serra spent the rest of his life walking and riding across California. Many areas had never been explored. He set up nine missions. They were located across 700 miles of land. He sent back reports about what he saw and found in the new country. In some places, the roads were rough and rocky. It was hard to ride on them. In other places, he found cool streams. He saw

riverbanks covered with roses. He found grapes growing wild. He met many American Indians. He said that they all treated him well.

In 1784, Father Serra was 70 years old. He had walked and ridden back and forth across California many times. It is thought that he traveled about 24,000 miles. This life of camping, walking, and riding was hard for him. He died at one of his missions. But, he had opened up new land. Much of early California was settled thanks to this explorer.

Father Junípero Serra
(1713–1784)

1. Choose a good title for this passage.

   a. The Priest Who Explored the New World

   b. Missions in Mexico

   c. The Good Student

   d. The Man Who Walked across Mexico

2. What does the word **frail** mean in the passage?

   a. strong

   b. healthy

   c. weak or ill

   d. afraid

3. Number the following events in the order they happened.

   _____ Father Serra asked to go to Mexico.

   _____ Father Serra became a priest.

   _____ Father Serra explored northern California.

   _____ Father Serra died at one of his missions.

   _____ Father Serra went to school on the island where he was born.

4. Answer the following questions.

   Why did it seem like teaching was a good job for Father Serra?

   _____

   _____

   How did Father Serra get to Mexico City, Mexico?

   _____

   _____

   Why did Father Serra first go to California?

   _____

   _____

   What health problems did Father Serra have?

   _____

5. What does it mean to "open up new land"?

   a. to unlock gates on fenced-in land

   b. to explore a new place so that others can go there

   c. to set up stores and homes so that people can move in

   d. to find something new about a place that is settled

Bonus

Look at a map of your region. Find a place about 200 miles from your home. What would it be like to walk there? How long do you think it would take?

María Gertrudis de la Garza Falcón
(1734–1789)

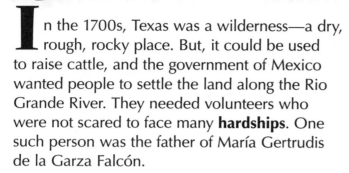

In the 1700s, Texas was a wilderness—a dry, rough, rocky place. But, it could be used to raise cattle, and the government of Mexico wanted people to settle the land along the Rio Grande River. They needed volunteers who were not scared to face many **hardships**. One such person was the father of María Gertrudis de la Garza Falcón.

María's father moved to Texas to build a ranch for his family and a village for settlers. María came to Texas with the rest of her family in 1750. Her father was given a huge piece of land—the largest ever granted in Texas. He controlled more than 900,000 acres. In exchange for this, María's family helped create a tiny settlement along the Rio Grande. Spanish soldiers camped on the ranch to keep everyone safe.

Only a year after María arrived, the whole village was destroyed in a flood. Everything had to be built again on higher ground, but the settlers did not give up. María chose to stay in this wild land, marrying a man named Salvador. Together, they asked the Mexican government for their own ranch land. They received a ranch that had about 250,000 acres. It was called Rancho Viejo.

At that time, ranches were like fortresses. The people living on them were in constant danger of attacks by local American Indian tribes. Ranchers built stone walls around their homes. The walls had small openings for guns. Deep wells provided water in case attacks went on for days. This was the kind of life that María and Salvador faced.

When Salvador died, María decided once again to stay in Texas. Many people at that time would have given up, but María did not. She could have moved back to Mexico, where life was much easier, but she had the heart of a genuine pioneer. She took over the ranch and ran it by herself.

María raised goats and sheep. The ranch also had cattle. The cattle that María raised had to be tough because they stayed in the hot sun all day. Sometimes, it did not rain for months at a time. María bred cattle that stood up to this hard life. Two hundred years later, the herds of cattle found in this part of Texas were used to create a new breed: Santa Gertrudis cattle. They are raised today on the huge King Ranch in Texas, which is located partly on land that was first settled by María Gertrudis's family.

María Gertrudis de la Garza Falcón
(1734–1789)

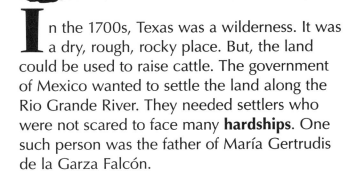

In the 1700s, Texas was a wilderness. It was a dry, rough, rocky place. But, the land could be used to raise cattle. The government of Mexico wanted to settle the land along the Rio Grande River. They needed settlers who were not scared to face many **hardships**. One such person was the father of María Gertrudis de la Garza Falcón.

María's father moved to Texas. He built a ranch for his family and a village for settlers. María moved to Texas with the rest of her family in 1750. Her father was given a huge piece of land—the largest ever given in Texas. He had more than 900,000 acres. The land was payment for the job he had to do. He helped make a settlement on the Rio Grande. Spanish soldiers camped on the ranch to keep everyone safe.

Only a year after María arrived, the whole village was ruined in a flood. Everything had to be built again on higher ground. But, the settlers did not give up. María stayed in this wild land. She married a man named Salvador. Together, they asked Mexico for their own ranch land. They got a ranch that had about 250,000 acres. It was called Rancho Viejo.

At that time, ranches were like forts. The people living there were in constant danger of attacks by local American Indian tribes. Ranchers built walls around their homes. The walls had small openings for guns. This was the kind of life that María and Salvador faced.

When Salvador died, María stayed in Texas. Many people at that time would have given up. But, María did not give up. She could have moved back to Mexico, where life was easier. But, she had the heart of a real pioneer. She took over the ranch. She ran it by herself.

The ranch had goats and sheep. It also had cattle. The cattle that María raised had to be tough. They stayed in the hot sun all day. Sometimes, it did not rain for months at a time. María bred cattle that stood up to this hard life. Two hundred years later, the herds of cattle found in this part of Texas were used to make a new breed. They are called Santa Gertrudis cattle. This is a breed raised today on the huge King Ranch in Texas. Part of the King Ranch is on land that was first settled by María Gertrudis's family.

María Gertrudis de la Garza Falcón
(1734–1789)

1. This passage is mainly about:

   a. the first woman to start a settlement in Mexico.

   b. a woman who became a pioneer and a rancher in Texas.

   c. a woman who lived in Texas with her family, then moved to Mexico.

   d. a young woman who grew up on a ranch but left to do other things.

2. What does the word **hardships** mean in the passage?

   a. vessels

   b. things that are easy

   c. difficulties

   d. pioneers

3. Number the following events in the order they happened.

   _____ María and Salvador got a land grant for a ranch.

   _____ María got married.

   _____ María died.

   _____ María took charge of Rancho Viejo.

   _____ María moved to Texas.

4. Answer the following questions.

   When did María move to Texas?

   _____

   What job did María's father do in Texas?

   _____

   _____

   What is one detail that shows how dangerous it was to live in Texas at that time?

   _____

   _____

   What did María do after her husband died?

   _____

   _____

5. What did María do on her ranch that helped people in the future?

   a. She started a breed of cattle that could live in the harsh climate.

   b. She blocked off a stream to make a lake.

   c. She kept soldiers on her land to keep it safe.

   d. Nobody knows what María did when she ran the ranch.

Bonus

Imagine that María kept a journal. Write an entry about one day of her life in Texas.

David Farragut's ninth year was an important one for him. It was the year in which he first went to sea. David's father was Spanish. He came to the United States in 1776. He was a brave soldier who fought for his new country in two wars: the American Revolution and the War of 1812. David's mother died when he was seven. David was sent to live with a navy captain named David Porter, and it was Porter who found a place on a ship for David.

David was at sea during all of the War of 1812. When he was only 12 years old, he was put in charge of a prize ship, a vessel that had been captured from the enemy. David's job was to get the ship safely back to port. This was a difficult job during a war, but David did it.

For many years after that, the country was peaceful and David's assignments for the navy were mainly desk jobs. Then, the Civil War started. David lived in Virginia. He loved the South and his home, but he told his wife he was "sticking to the flag." So, David and his wife moved to New York. He was 60 years old. Most men would have stopped working by then, but the most exciting and challenging part of David's life was just beginning.

The North could not use the Mississippi River because it was so well protected. David was asked to **capture** New Orleans, Louisiana, an important port for the South and the gateway to the huge river system. David commanded his flagship, the *Hartford*. He had almost 50 other ships with him. Using their 200 cannons, David blasted at the forts that defended New Orleans. The city fell, and David was a hero in the North.

David helped capture cities up and down the Mississippi River. Then, he turned to Mobile, Alabama. The year was 1864, and Mobile was the last big port that the South held in its control. Once again, David blasted his way through. His ship led the way and was under heavy fire. In less than two years, the *Hartford* was hit 240 times by cannon fire. But, David kept going no matter what he faced during combat.

By this time, the war was almost over. David was ill and tired. He went home to New York. He was made an admiral by the navy for the important work he did to help win the Civil War for the North.

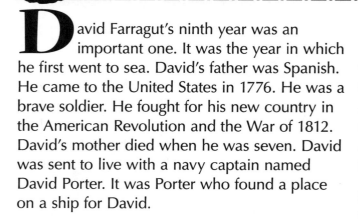

David Glasgow Farragut
(1801–1870)

David Farragut's ninth year was an important one. It was the year in which he first went to sea. David's father was Spanish. He came to the United States in 1776. He was a brave soldier. He fought for his new country in the American Revolution and the War of 1812. David's mother died when he was seven. David was sent to live with a navy captain named David Porter. It was Porter who found a place on a ship for David.

David was at sea during all of the War of 1812. When he was only 12 years old, he was put in charge of a prize ship. This was a ship that had been captured from the enemy. David's job was to get the ship safely back to port. This was a hard job during a war, but David did it.

For many years after that, the country was peaceful. David mainly had desk jobs. Then, the Civil War started. David lived in Virginia. He loved the South and his home. But, he told his wife that he was "sticking to the flag." So, David and his wife moved to New York. He was 60 years old. Most men would have stopped working by then. But, the most exciting part of David's life was just starting.

The North could not use the Mississippi River because it was so well guarded. David was asked to **capture** New Orleans, Louisiana. This was an important port for the South. It was the gateway to the huge river system. David went on his flagship, the *Hartford*. He had almost 50 other ships with him. Using their 200 cannons, David blasted at the forts that kept New Orleans safe. The city fell. David was a hero in the North.

David helped capture cities on the Mississippi River. Then, he turned to Mobile, Alabama. The year was 1864. Mobile was the last big port that the South had. Once again, David blasted his way through. His ship led the way and was under heavy fire. In less than two years, the *Hartford* was hit 240 times by cannon fire. But, David kept going no matter what.

By this time, the war was almost over. David was ill and tired. He went home to New York. He was made an admiral for the important work he did to help win the Civil War for the North.

David Glasgow Farragut
(1801–1870)

1. The last paragraph is mainly about:

   a. David's command during the Civil War.

   b. David's childhood.

   c. how David went to sea for the first time.

   d. how David was rewarded for his Civil War service.

2. What does the word **capture** mean in the passage?

   a. to take control of

   b. to guard

   c. to keep safe

   d. to clothe

3. Number the following events in the order they happened.

   _____ David brought a captured ship safely to port.

   _____ David captured the port of Mobile, Alabama.

   _____ David's mother died.

   _____ David was sent to live with a navy captain.

   _____ David fought battles on the Mississippi River.

4. Answer the following questions.

   Who was David Porter?

   _____

   _____

   What city did David have to capture to get to the Mississippi River?

   _____

   How many times was David's ship hit by cannon fire?

   _____

   What rank was David given at the end of the war?

   _____

5. What did David mean when he told his wife that he was "sticking to the flag"?

   a. He wanted to fight for the South.

   b. He would not go against the Union, so he would fight for the North.

   c. He would not fight for either side.

   d. He wanted a flag for his ship.

Bonus

Look at the Mississippi River on a map. Then, write a paragraph explaining why it would be important to control New Orleans, Louisiana, if you wanted to use the river for shipping.

Hispanic American Achievers   © Carson-Dellosa • CD-104256

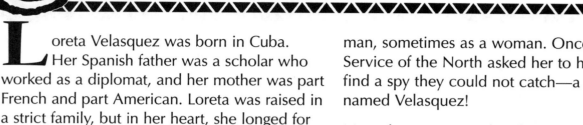

Loreta Velasquez was born in Cuba. Her Spanish father was a scholar who worked as a diplomat, and her mother was part French and part American. Loreta was raised in a strict family, but in her heart, she longed for freedom and adventure.

So, Loreta ran away and married a soldier. They went to the United States just before the start of the Civil War. Her husband was sent to serve in the army for the South, and Loreta wanted to be with him. She went to a tailor shop and had uniforms made. Then, she padded the uniforms to hide her shape. She cut her hair, glued on a fake beard, and traveled south to be with her husband.

During her trip, Loreta stopped in several places. She formed a regiment of soldiers and marched them to Florida. Her husband was shocked by what she did, but he died before he could send her home.

Loreta chose to remain a soldier. She fought in the first major battle of the war, the First Battle of Bull Run. Then, she fought in other battles, as well.

While helping bury the dead after a battle, Loreta was shot in the foot. An army doctor found out that she was really a woman. She was arrested and had to pay a fine. After she was set free, she bought another uniform, went back to the army, and **enlisted** again.

Loreta was just in time to fight in the battle of Shiloh. She fought with a man she later married. She was wounded again and had to confess to the doctor that she was really a woman. Since she could no longer fight, Loreta decided to become a spy for the South. She went on many secret missions. Sometimes she dressed as a man, sometimes as a woman. Once, the Secret Service of the North asked her to help them find a spy they could not catch—a woman named Velasquez!

More than 10 years after the war ended, Loreta wrote a book about her adventures. It was called *A Woman in Battle*. It is hard today to tell if everything in the book is true. Loreta wrote that she met President Abraham Lincoln. She said that she had a chance to shoot General Ulysses S. Grant but she could not bring herself to do it. She wrote about her daring spy missions and thrilling adventures in battle. She may have stretched the truth so that she could tell exciting stories. But, many people believe that she was a soldier. Her tales of battles sound true and are full of details. And, even if Loreta did only half of the things she wrote about, she was still a true hero of the Civil War.

Loreta Janeta Velasquez
(1842?–1897?)

Loreta Velasquez was born in Cuba. Her Spanish father was an educated man. He worked as a diplomat. Her mother was part French and part American. Loreta was raised in a strict family. But in her heart, she longed for freedom. She wanted adventure.

Loreta ran away with a soldier. They got married and went to the United States. Then, the Civil War started. Her husband was sent to serve in the army for the South. Loreta wanted to be with him. She went to a tailor shop. She had uniforms made. Then, she padded the uniforms to hide her shape. She cut her hair. She glued on a fake beard. Then, she went south to be with her husband.

On her trip, Loreta stopped in several places. She formed a regiment of soldiers. She marched them to Florida. Her husband was shocked by what she did. But, he died before he could send her home.

Loreta chose to stay a soldier. She fought in the first big battle of the war, the First Battle of Bull Run. She fought in other battles, too.

Then, Loreta was shot in the foot. She was helping bury the dead after a battle. An army doctor found out that she was a woman. She was arrested. She had to pay a fine. After she was freed, she bought another uniform. She went back to the army and **enlisted** again.

Loreta was just in time to fight in the battle of Shiloh. She fought with a man whom she later married. She was wounded again and had to tell the doctor that she was really a woman. Since she could no longer fight, Loreta decided to become a spy for the South. She went on many missions. Sometimes she dressed as a man, and sometimes she dressed as a woman. Once, the Secret Service of the North asked her to help them find the female spy named Velasquez!

More than 10 years after the war ended, Loreta wrote a book about her adventures. It was called *A Woman in Battle*. It is hard today to tell if everything in the book is true. Loreta wrote that she met President Abraham Lincoln. She said that she had a chance to shoot General Ulysses S. Grant but she could not do it. She wrote about her many spy missions and adventures in battle. She may have stretched the truth to tell exciting stories. But, many people believe that she was a soldier. Her tales of battles seem to be true and full of details. And, even if Loreta did only half of the things she wrote about, she was still a true hero of the Civil War.

Loreta Janeta Velasquez
(1842?–1897?)

1. The second paragraph is mainly about:

   a. Loreta's parents.

   b. Loreta's decision to become a spy.

   c. how Loreta planned to be close to her husband, a soldier.

   d. how Loreta went on spy missions.

2. What does the word **enlisted** mean in the passage?

   a. found a list of supplies or equipment

   b. made a list of the battles she was in

   c. wrote very fast

   d. signed up to be in the military

3. Number the following events in the order they happened.

   _____ Loreta was born in Cuba.

   _____ Loreta ran away with a soldier to the United States.

   _____ Loreta gave up being a soldier and became a spy.

   _____ Loreta stayed to fight as a soldier after her husband died.

   _____ Loreta marched a regiment to Florida.

4. Answer the following questions.

   Whom did Loreta claim that she almost shot?

   _____

   Why did Loreta buy uniforms and dress like a man?

   _____

   _____

   What was the first battle in which Loreta fought?

   _____

   In what battle was Loreta wounded for the second time?

   _____

5. Why does the author say that some of Loreta's book might have been made up and some of it might be true?

   a. Loreta wanted to tell thrilling stories.

   b. Some of the stories, like meeting President Lincoln, seem like they might not be true.

   c. Loreta wrote about battles as if she had been there, with a lot of details.

   d. all of the above

Bonus

Write a story about one of Loreta's spy missions. What kind of information would she want to find out about the other side? How would she find this information? How would she keep from getting caught?

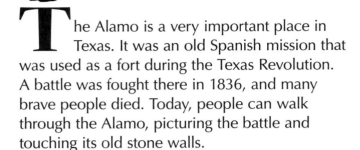

Adina De Zavala
(1861–1955)

The Alamo is a very important place in Texas. It was an old Spanish mission that was used as a fort during the Texas Revolution. A battle was fought there in 1836, and many brave people died. Today, people can walk through the Alamo, picturing the battle and touching its old stone walls.

It is difficult to imagine that people wanted to tear down part of the Alamo. But in 1908, a group wanted to transform the Alamo into a park. They wanted to tear down the old walls and part of the fort. But, one woman stood in their way, a woman who saved the Alamo.

That woman was Adina De Zavala. Adina was from an old Texan family. She was raised on a ranch, where she loved to read books about history. Adina became a teacher. When she learned about the plan to demolish the Alamo, she hired three men to go there and send away the workers who were going to tear it down. Instead, the workers chased away the three men.

But, Adina had a backup plan. The workers did not know that Adina was there too, barricaded inside the old building. She would not move. She lived there for three days. Nobody could tear down the walls while she was inside.

Later, Adina said that she knew she had to "hold the fort." She did it for the soldiers who had fought there in 1836, to preserve their memory.

People around the country heard about Adina's brave action. Someone even wrote a song about saving the Alamo, with Adina's picture on the sheet music!

The Alamo was not the only building that Adina saved. She saved four other Spanish missions. She kept people from tearing down the huge palace where Spanish **governors** used to live. She raised money to put up historical markers around the state, showing where events in history had taken place.

Adina wrote about history, too. She wrote a book about the Alamo. She wrote many articles, as well as plays and stories for children. A lot of Adina's ideas about teaching Texas history are still used in schools today. Thanks to her, we can enjoy the rich and interesting history of this immense state.

Hispanic American Achievers   © Carson-Dellosa • CD-104256

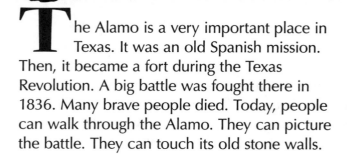

The Alamo is a very important place in Texas. It was an old Spanish mission. Then, it became a fort during the Texas Revolution. A big battle was fought there in 1836. Many brave people died. Today, people can walk through the Alamo. They can picture the battle. They can touch its old stone walls.

It is hard to think that people wanted to tear down part of the Alamo. But in 1908, a group wanted to make the Alamo into a park. They wanted to tear down the old walls and part of the fort. But, one woman stood in their way. She saved the Alamo.

That woman was Adina De Zavala. Adina was from an old Texan family. She was raised on a ranch. She loved to read books about history. Adina became a teacher. One day, she found out about a plan to tear down the Alamo. So, she hired three men to go there. She wanted them to send away the workers who were going to tear down the Alamo. Instead, the workers chased away the three men.

But, Adina had another plan. The workers did not know that Adina was inside the old building. She would not move. She lived there for three days. Nobody could tear down the walls while she was inside.

Later, Adina said that she knew she had to "hold the fort." She did it for the soldiers who had fought there in 1836.

People around the country heard about Adina's brave act. Someone even wrote a song about saving the Alamo. Adina's picture was on the sheet music!

The Alamo was not the only building that Adina saved. She saved four other Spanish missions. She kept people from tearing down the huge home where Spanish **governors** used to live. She raised money to put up markers around the state. The markers showed where events in history had taken place.

Adina wrote about history, too. She wrote a book about the Alamo. She wrote many articles. She wrote plays and stories for children. A lot of Adina's ideas about teaching Texas history are still used in schools today. Thanks to her, we can enjoy the rich and interesting history of this huge state.

Adina De Zavala
(1861–1955)

1. The second paragraph is mainly about:

   a. Adina's childhood.

   b. how Adina saved the Alamo.

   c. how a group planned to tear down the Alamo.

   d. Adina's writing.

2. What does the word **governors** mean in the passage?

   a. leaders or commanders who rule over a place

   b. people who ask the citizens how they want a place run

   c. people who have the right to vote

   d. leaders of sports teams

3. Number the following events in the order they happened.

   _____ A group planned to tear down part of the Alamo to make a park.

   _____ Adina grew up on a ranch.

   _____ Adina lived inside the Alamo for three days.

   _____ Someone wrote a song about Adina.

   _____ Adina became a teacher.

4. Answer the following questions.

   What is the Alamo?

   _____

   _____

   What was the subject of the book Adina wrote?

   _____

   _____

   What do the markers that Adina helped put up in Texas do?

   _____

   _____

   What does it mean to "hold the fort"?

   _____

   _____

5. Why weren't the workers able to tear down the Alamo while Adina was locked inside?

   a. If they tore down the walls, Adina would cry.

   b. The workers were afraid of Adina.

   c. If they tore down the walls, Adina might get hurt.

   d. The workers were paid by Adina.

Bonus

Have you ever visited or seen pictures of a place that was important in history? Write a paragraph about it. Remember to use words that show how it looks, feels, smells, and sounds. Use your imagination if you have never visited the place.

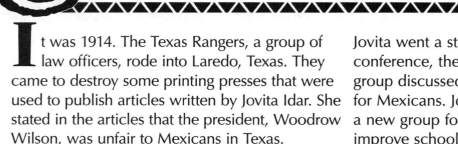

Jovita Idar
(1885–1946)

It was 1914. The Texas Rangers, a group of law officers, rode into Laredo, Texas. They came to destroy some printing presses that were used to publish articles written by Jovita Idar. She stated in the articles that the president, Woodrow Wilson, was unfair to Mexicans in Texas.

The Rangers were used to people being scared of them. But, in the doorway of the newspaper office stood a young woman. She planted her feet on the step and braced herself with her arms. She was not going to move. The Rangers turned and rode away.

The Rangers came back at night. They broke into the office and smashed everything. But, few people forgot how Jovita had stood up to them.

The years between 1910 and 1921 were hard ones for Texas. A war was being fought in Mexico. Many people tried to escape from the fighting. They crossed into Texas, but the people in Texas did not want them there. Some of the Mexicans were put to death. Even children were not safe.

Jovita's father owned a Spanish-language newspaper called *La Crónica*. Jovita trained to be a teacher, but she taught Mexican children and could not get the books and supplies she needed. So, she quit in 1910 and started to write for her father's newspaper instead.

It was dangerous to speak out against the Texans and to criticize the United States government. But, Jovita did both. She wrote about the unfair treatment of Mexicans in Texas. She wrote about the revolution in Mexico. She wrote about the illegal ways that the Texas Rangers enforced the law. In 1911,

Jovita went a step further. She called for a big conference, the First Mexican Congress. The group discussed schools, jobs, and life in Texas for Mexicans. Jovita used the congress to form a new group for women. This group helped improve schools for Mexican children.

But, that work was not enough for Jovita. She also helped **launch** *La Cruz Blanca*, the White Cross. This group of nurses took care of people who were hurt in the war in Mexico. When Jovita was not writing for the newspaper, she crossed the border to serve as a nurse. In 1914, her father died. So, Jovita ran the newspaper by herself.

Jovita got married in 1917. She moved with her husband to San Antonio, Texas. The Mexican Revolution ended in 1921, but this did not bring an end to Jovita's work. She set up a free kindergarten for Mexican children, worked in a hospital, and edited a magazine. She spent her whole life helping make life better for others.

Jovita Idar
(1885–1946)

It was 1914. The Texas Rangers, a group of law officers, rode into Laredo, Texas. They came to shut down some printing presses. The presses printed articles written by Jovita Idar. She said that the president, Woodrow Wilson, was unfair to Mexicans in Texas.

The Rangers were used to people being scared of them. But, a young woman stood in the doorway of the newspaper office. She planted her feet on the step. She braced herself with her arms. She was not going to move. The Rangers turned and rode away.

The Rangers came back at night. They smashed everything in the office. But, few people forgot how Jovita had stood up to them.

The years between 1910 and 1921 were hard ones for Texas. A war was going on in Mexico. Many people tried to run away from the fighting. They came to Texas. But, the people in Texas did not want them there. Some of the Mexicans were put to death. Even children were not safe.

Jovita's father owned a newspaper called *La Crónica*. It was written in Spanish. Jovita trained to be a teacher. She taught Mexican children. But, she could not get the books and supplies she needed for them. So, she quit in 1910. She started to write for her father's newspaper.

It was not safe to speak out against the Texans or to criticize the United States government. But, Jovita did both. She wrote about the unfair treatment of Mexicans in Texas. She wrote about the revolution in Mexico. She wrote about how the Texas Rangers did illegal things

to enforce the laws. In 1911, Jovita went a step further. She called for a big meeting, the First Mexican Congress. The group talked about schools, jobs, and life in Texas for Mexicans. Jovita used the congress to start a new group for women. This group helped make schools better for Mexican children.

But, that work was not enough for Jovita. She also helped **launch** *La Cruz Blanca*, the White Cross. This group of nurses took care of people who were hurt in the war in Mexico. When Jovita was not writing for the newspaper, she crossed the border to serve as a nurse. In 1914, her father died. So, Jovita ran the newspaper by herself.

Jovita got married in 1917. She moved with her husband to San Antonio, Texas. The Mexican Revolution ended in 1921, but Jovita did not stop her work. She set up a free kindergarten for Mexican children. She worked in a hospital. She worked on a magazine. She spent her whole life helping make life better for others.

Jovita Idar
(1885–1946)

1. What is the main idea of this passage?

    a. Jovita Idar was a teacher.

    b. Jovita Idar was a brave woman who worked to help Mexicans in Texas.

    c. Jovita Idar was the first woman to write for a newspaper.

    d. Jovita Idar was a writer.

2. What does the word **launch** mean in the passage?

    a. to put something in the water

    b. to push something into outer space

    c. to start something new

    d. to make something explode

3. Number the following events in the order they happened.

    _____ Jovita Idar trained to be a teacher.

    _____ Jovita set up a free kindergarten in San Antonio, Texas.

    _____ Jovita started to work with her father on *La Crónica*.

    _____ Jovita crossed into Mexico to serve as a nurse.

    _____ Jovita called for the First Mexican Congress.

4. Answer the following questions.

    What was *La Crónica*?

    _____

    _____

    How did Jovita stand up to the Texas Rangers?

    _____

    _____

    Why did Mexicans cross into Texas between 1910 and 1921?

    _____

    _____

    Name one group that Jovita started during the Mexican Revolution.

    _____

5. What was *La Cruz Blanca*?

    a. It was a group that helped make schools better for Mexican children.

    b. It was a big meeting in which people talked about jobs and schools in Texas.

    c. It was a group of soldiers who went to fight in Mexico.

    d. It was a group of nurses who crossed into Mexico to help people who were hurt in the war.

Bonus

Write a paragraph that compares and contrasts Jovita Idar's work to the work of another civil rights leader, such as Martin Luther King Jr.

Marcelino Serna
(1896–1992)

Marcelino Serna was born in Mexico. Like many others, he came to the United States as a teenager to look for work. Marcelino found a job working for a railroad company in 1916. Later, he got a job working on a farm in Colorado.

World War I started. The government was drafting soldiers to fight in Europe. Marcelino was picked up in 1917 by a government official who had to check to see if Marcelino was eligible to fight. Marcelino knew that the official would find out that he was not an American citizen. He did not have to go to war, but Marcelino **volunteered** to go. He was 20 years old.

The young soldier was given only three weeks of training. Then, he was sent to England. From there, his company went to France to fight. When Marcelino arrived in France, an officer came to see him. He told Marcelino that the army had made an error and discovered that Marcelino was actually from Mexico. He told Marcelino that the army would pay for him to go home if he wanted to. Marcelino replied that he wanted to stay and help.

His company went to the Argonne Forest, where some of the worst fighting of the war happened. One day, the soldiers in Marcelino's company were marching when they were surprised by a nest of German machine guns. The Americans were trapped by the gunfire.

Marcelino volunteered to go by himself to capture the Germans. He ran, dropped to the ground, and ran again. Bullets struck his helmet, but he did not stop. He blew up the guns and captured eight German soldiers, saving the rest of his company.

During another battle, Marcelino again proved his bravery. He spotted a lone gunman and wounded him. Then, he followed the limping German to discover where his company was hiding. Marcelino had only a rifle and a few grenades, but he kept moving, firing from different positions. He made the Germans think that there were many soldiers attacking them. He captured 24 soldiers that day.

Marcelino fought for months like this without once getting hurt. Then, one day in battle, he was shot in both legs. It was only four days before the end of the war. When the war ended in 1918, Marcelino was in a hospital in France.

Marcelino was awarded many medals for his brave fighting. France, Italy, England, and the United States all gave him medals, making him one of the most decorated soldiers of the war. After the war, Marcelino traveled back to the United States. He became a citizen in 1924, six years after fighting so bravely for his adopted country.

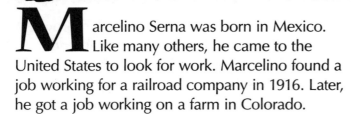

Marcelino Serna
(1896–1992)

Marcelino Serna was born in Mexico. Like many others, he came to the United States to look for work. Marcelino found a job working for a railroad company in 1916. Later, he got a job working on a farm in Colorado.

World War I started. The government was drafting soldiers to fight in Europe. Marcelino was picked up in 1917 by a government officer who was checking to see if he could be sent to fight. Marcelino knew that the man would find out that he was not an American citizen. He did not have to go to war. But, Marcelino **volunteered** to go. He was 20 years old.

The young soldier was given only three weeks of training. Then, he was sent to England. His company went to France to fight. When Marcelino got to France, an officer came to see him. He told Marcelino that the army had made a mistake. They found out that Marcelino was from Mexico. He could go home if he wanted to. The army would pay to send him home. Marcelino told the officer that he wanted to stay and help.

His company went to the Argonne Forest. This was where some of the worst fighting of the war happened. One day, the soldiers were marching. They were surprised by a nest of German machine guns. The Americans were trapped.

Marcelino said that he would go by himself to capture the Germans. He ran, dropped to the ground, and ran again. Bullets hit his helmet. But, he did not stop. He blew up the guns and captured eight German soldiers. He saved the rest of his company.

During another battle, Marcelino again showed how brave he was. He spotted a lone gunman and wounded him. Then, he followed the German to find out where his company was hiding. Marcelino had only a rifle and a few grenades. But, he kept moving. He made the Germans think that there were many soldiers attacking them. He captured 24 soldiers that day.

Marcelino fought for months like this without getting hurt. Then, one day in battle, he was shot in both legs. It was only four days before the end of the war. When the war ended in 1918, Marcelino was in a hospital in France.

Marcelino was given many medals for his brave fighting. France, Italy, England, and the United States all gave him medals, making him one of the most honored soldiers of the war. After the war, Marcelino went back to the United States. He became a citizen in 1924, six years after fighting so bravely for his adopted country.

Marcelino Serna
(1896–1992)

1. Choose a good title for this passage.

   a. World War I Soldiers

   b. Becoming a Citizen of the United States

   c. Coming to the United States to Work

   d. A Brave Soldier and His Adopted Country

2. What does the word **volunteered** mean in the passage?

   a. withdrew

   b. pretended

   c. foiled

   d. offered

3. Number the following events in the order they happened.

   _____ Marcelino captured a machine-gun nest and eight German soldiers.

   _____ Marcelino trained for three weeks as a soldier.

   _____ Marcelino was told that the army would pay to send him home from France.

   _____ Marcelino captured 24 German soldiers in one day.

   _____ Marcelino worked for a railroad company in the United States.

4. Answer the following questions.

   Where was Marcelino born?

   _____

   Why didn't Marcelino have to fight for the United States?

   _____

   _____

   Where was Marcelino's company sent to fight?

   _____

   Which countries gave Marcelino medals for his bravery during World War I?

   _____

   _____

5. Which of the following details shows Marcelino's bravery?

   a. He had two chances to stay out of the war and turned them down.

   b. He said that he would capture a machine-gun nest all by himself.

   c. He was given medals by four different countries.

   d. all of the above

Bonus

The United States was not Marcelino's country, and he did not have to fight for it. Why do you think he chose to do so? Write a paragraph that explains your answer.

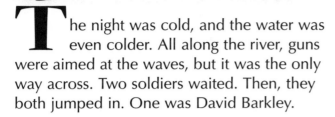

The night was cold, and the water was even colder. All along the river, guns were aimed at the waves, but it was the only way across. Two soldiers waited. Then, they both jumped in. One was David Barkley.

David was born in Laredo, Texas. His mother was Mexican American. When World War I started, David was a teenager. When America entered the war, David signed up to be a soldier. He was afraid that if the army found out that he was Hispanic American, they would put him in a segregated unit and he would not be allowed to fight. So, David kept his **background** a secret. His English-sounding name and blue eyes helped him keep his secret.

David was sent to France in 1918. His unit fought near the Meuse River, a place where the fighting was heaviest at the end of the war.

The soldiers needed to cross the river in order to fight the German army. But first, they needed to learn everything they could about the German army's troop strength and where they were located. Someone had to cross the river to spy on them.

David volunteered to go. A soldier named Waldo Hatler said that he would go with him. There was no bridge. The two young soldiers would have to swim across the deep, wide river. It was November, and the water was frigid.

David and Waldo set out on their mission. They made it across the river. Wet and shivering, they crept past the German soldiers. They counted the German troops, saw where the guns were placed, and found where the soldiers would be in the fight to come.

Then, it was time to swim back. David swam as hard as he could, but his muscles cramped. He went under the water and drowned before he could get to the other shore of the river. Waldo had the information that they had gathered, which helped the troops in their last fight of the war. Two days later, a peace agreement was signed.

General John J. Pershing, the officer in charge of all of the American soldiers fighting in World War I, praised David's bravery. David was given a hero's farewell in Texas. He was buried in the graveyard next to the Alamo, a famed Texas battle site.

David's courage also earned him several medals. He was awarded medals from France and Italy. He also earned the Medal of Honor, the highest award that the United States can give to a soldier.

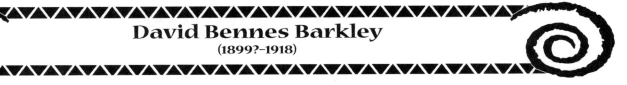

The night was cold. The water was even colder. All along the river, guns were aimed at the waves. But, it was the only way across. Two soldiers waited. Then, they both jumped in. One was David Barkley.

David was born in Laredo, Texas. His mother was Mexican American. David was in his teens when World War I started. David signed up to be a soldier. But, he was worried. If the army found out that he was Hispanic American, they would put him in a unit that would not be sent to fight. So, David did not tell the army about his **background**. His English-sounding name and blue eyes helped him keep his secret.

David was sent to France in 1918. His unit fought near the Meuse River. That was where the fighting was heaviest at the end of the war.

The soldiers needed to cross the river so that they could fight the German army. But first, they had to learn everything they could. They had to find out how many men the German army had. They had to find out where the German troops had machine guns. Someone had to cross the river to spy.

David said that he would go. A soldier named Waldo Hatler said that he would go, too. There was no bridge. The two young soldiers would have to swim across the deep, wide river. It was November. The water was very cold.

David and Waldo made it across the river. Wet and cold, they sneaked past the German soldiers. They counted the troops. They saw where the guns were placed. They found where the soldiers waited to fight.

Then, it was time to swim back. David swam as hard as he could. But, his muscles cramped. He went under the water. David drowned. He did not make it to the other side of the river. But, Waldo had the information that they had gathered. This helped the troops in their last fight of the war. Two days later, a peace agreement was signed.

David's brave act was praised by General John J. Pershing. He was the officer in charge of all of the American soldiers fighting in World War I. David was treated like a hero. He was buried next to the Alamo, a well-known Texas battle site.

David was also given medals in honor of his bravery. He got medals from France and Italy. He also earned the Medal of Honor. This is the highest honor that the United States can give to a soldier.

David Bennes Barkley
(1899?–1918)

1. What is the main idea of the fourth paragraph?

    a. David Barkley hid the secret that he was Hispanic American.

    b. The American soldiers had to learn more about the German troops before they could fight.

    c. David died trying to swim across the Meuse River.

    d. David was honored as a hero after his death.

2. What does the word **background** mean in the passage?

    a. scenery in the back of a painting

    b. hilly or rocky ground

    c. information about a person's family and past

    d. music that is played in a store

3. Number the following events in the order they happened.

    _____ World War I started.

    _____ David was sent to France to fight.

    _____ David signed up to be a soldier.

    _____ David was born in Texas.

    _____ David volunteered to go on a spy mission.

4. Answer the following questions.

    Where was David Barkley born?

    _____

    Why did David hide the fact that his mother was Mexican American?

    _____

    _____

    Name one thing that David had to find out about the German soldiers.

    _____

    _____

    Who praised David's brave act?

    _____

5. Why do you think the army needed to know how many German troops there were?

    a. The army needed to know how many gifts to bring to the German troops.

    b. It would help the army know how many American troops to send to fight on the other side of the river.

    c. The army wanted to be as prepared as possible for battle.

    d. b and c

Bonus

Read more about the Medal of Honor. Then, write a paragraph explaining why this medal was given to David Barkley.

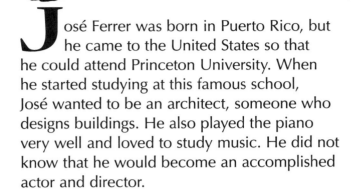

José Vicente Ferrer de Otero y Cintrón
(1909?–1992)

José Ferrer was born in Puerto Rico, but he came to the United States so that he could attend Princeton University. When he started studying at this famous school, José wanted to be an architect, someone who designs buildings. He also played the piano very well and loved to study music. He did not know that he would become an accomplished actor and director.

In fact, José did not act in a play until the year after he graduated from college. But once he started acting, he did not want to stop.

José moved to New York City and started to act in plays on Broadway. In 1940, he starred in a hit play. By 1952, he had won three Tony® Awards. Two of the awards were for acting. The other award was for directing. José loved creating whole stories as a director, as well as creating individual characters as an actor.

In 1948, José started to play parts in movies. He won an Oscar® in 1950 for his portrayal of Cyrano, a man who thinks that he is too ugly to be loved by the woman he cares for. So, Cyrano helps another man win her love instead.

José played the part of another tragic man in 1952. He made a film about Henri de Toulouse-Lautrec. Henri was a French artist. As a teenager, he broke his legs, and they stopped growing. So, Henri was only 4 feet 6 inches tall as an adult. José was very tall. How could he play the artist? José decided to play the part on his knees. He made special pads for his knees so that he could walk on them. It was very painful, and he could do only a few minutes of a scene at a time. The movie won two Oscars®.

José had so many interests that it was difficult for him to devote enough time to them all. He had a beautiful voice. He sang the lead part in *Man of La Mancha*, a musical about a Spanish author and the character he creates for a novel. José directed movies and plays. And, he acted throughout his life.

One of the most important moments of José's life came in 1985. Congress created a new honor for artists and actors, an award called the National Medal of Arts. José was the first actor to be given this medal, which he received for his lifetime of work onstage and in films.

José was not the only member of his family with a **career** in show business. José was married to a popular singer named Rosemary Clooney. They had five children. Two of their sons, Miguel Ferrer and Rafael Ferrer, are actors today. So is José's nephew, George Clooney.

José Vicente Ferrer de Otero y Cintrón
(1909?–1992)

José Ferrer was born in Puerto Rico. But, he came to the United States to go to Princeton University. When he started studying at this well-known school, José wanted to be an architect, someone who designs buildings. He also played the piano very well and loved to study music. He did not know that he would become an actor and a director.

In fact, José did not act in a play until the year after he finished college. But, once he started acting, he did not want to stop.

José went to New York City. He started to act in plays on Broadway. In 1940, he starred in a hit play. By 1952, he had won three Tony® Awards. Two were for acting. The other was for directing. José loved to create stories as a director, as well as characters as an actor.

In 1948, José started to play parts in movies. He won an Oscar® in 1950 for playing Cyrano, a man who thinks that he is too ugly to be loved by the woman he cares for. So, Cyrano helps another man win her love instead.

José played the part of another man in 1952. He made a film about Henri de Toulouse-Lautrec. Henri was a French artist. As a teenager, he broke his legs, and they stopped growing. This meant that Henri was only 4 feet 6 inches tall. José was very tall. How could he play the artist? José chose to play the part on his knees. He made special pads for his knees so that he could walk on them. It was very painful. He could do only a few minutes of a scene at a time. The movie won two Oscars®.

José had so many interests that it was hard for him to find enough time for all of them. He had a beautiful voice. He sang the lead part in the musical *Man of La Mancha*. It is about a Spanish author and the character he creates for a book. José directed movies and plays. And, he acted throughout his life.

One of the most important moments of José's life came in 1985. Congress created a new honor for artists and actors. It was a medal called the National Medal of Arts. José was the first actor to be given this medal. It was for his lifetime of work onstage and in films.

José was not the only person in his family with a **career** in show business. He was married to a singer named Rosemary Clooney. They had five children. Two of their sons, Miguel Ferrer and Rafael Ferrer, are actors today. So is José's nephew, George Clooney.

José Vicente Ferrer de Otero y Cintrón
(1909?–1992)

1. Choose a good title for this passage.

   a. Winning the National Medal of Arts

   b. From Puerto Rico to Princeton

   c. A Man of Many Talents

   d. The Life of an Actor

2. What does the word **career** mean in the passage?

   a. what a person does in his spare time

   b. what a person does as a job

   c. what a person does during retirement

   d. what a person does as a child

3. Number the following events in the order they happened.

   _____ José acted in his first Broadway play.

   _____ José won an Oscar® for playing Cyrano.

   _____ José was given the National Medal of Arts.

   _____ José played the part of a French artist in a film.

   _____ José attended college in the United States.

4. Answer the following questions.

   Why did José come to the United States?

   _____

   _____

   When did José act in his first play?

   _____

   In what musical did José sing the lead part?

   _____

   Name one thing that José did in addition to acting.

   _____

5. Why did José find it hard to give enough time to all of his interests?

   a. He was good at so many things that there was not time for all of them.

   b. He wanted to spend more time acting in plays, but he did not get the parts.

   c. He had so many talents that he had to give up some of them.

   d. none of the above

Bonus

What is your biggest talent? Think about the thing you do best. Is it also something you love doing? Write about this talent and why you enjoy it or why you do not enjoy it.

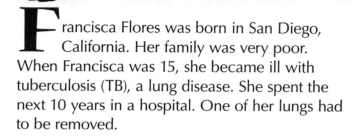

Francisca Flores
(1913–1996)

Francisca Flores was born in San Diego, California. Her family was very poor. When Francisca was 15, she became ill with tuberculosis (TB), a lung disease. She spent the next 10 years in a hospital. One of her lungs had to be removed.

But, there was a positive side to her illness. Francisca met many people in the hospital who had come to the United States from Mexico. She learned about the history of Mexico and the recent revolution. Her friends told her about the **struggles** of Mexicans in the United States. She wanted to know more, and she wanted to find ways to help.

Francisca was cured of TB around the time that World War II started. Another kind of war was raging in Los Angeles, California. It began for Francisca with the Sleepy Lagoon trial.

In 1942, many Hispanic Americans were forbidden from using the public swimming pools in Los Angeles. So, many young people swam at a place called Sleepy Lagoon. One hot summer night, two groups of teens got into a fight there. When the clash ended, a man was dead. His name was José Diaz. He had just joined the army and was about to go to war.

The police used the death as an excuse to put hundreds of people in jail. Most of them were Hispanic Americans, and most of them had nothing to do with the fight or the death. Twenty-two young men were put on trial. There was no definite proof that José was killed on purpose, but 12 young men were found guilty of murder.

Francisca asked to help with the case. She worked with a group that tried to get the facts of

the case printed in newspapers and aired on the radio. She wanted to help show how badly the Mexican Americans had been treated and how their civil rights had been taken away. This work marked the start of her career as a writer. For the rest of her life, Francisca wrote articles and helped edit Spanish-language magazines.

In the 1950s, Francisca worked with the unions as they helped workers. Around that time, a movie was made. It was called *Salt of the Earth*, and it told the story of a strike at a mine where many Hispanic Americans worked. The government did not like the film's message and made it against the law to watch it. But, Francisca planned secret meetings where people could come, watch the movie, and discuss the strike.

In the 1960s, Francisca praised Dr. Martin Luther King Jr. for his civil rights work, telling other Hispanic Americans that they should march with him. In the 1970s, Francisca was voted the first president of a new committee for women's rights. The group ran a center to help Hispanic women learn new skills and find jobs. Francisca was always proud of her Hispanic American background. She wanted her people to be a bridge between the Americas, and her work showed the way.

Francisca Flores
(1913–1996)

Francisca Flores was born in San Diego, California. Her family was very poor. When Francisca was 15, she became ill with tuberculosis (TB). She spent the next 10 years in a hospital. One of her lungs had to be taken out.

But, there was a good side to her illness. Francisca met many people in the hospital who were from Mexico. She learned about the history of Mexico. Her friends told her about the **struggles** of Mexicans in the United States. She wanted to know more. She wanted to help.

Francisca got better around the time that World War II started. Another kind of war started, too. It was in Los Angeles, California. It started for Francisca with the Sleepy Lagoon trial.

In 1942, many Hispanic Americans could not use the public swimming pools in Los Angeles. So, many young people swam at a place called Sleepy Lagoon. One hot summer night, two groups of teens got into a fight there. When the fight ended, a man was dead. His name was José Diaz. He had just joined the army. He was about to go to war.

The police put hundreds of people in jail. Most of them were Hispanic Americans. Most of them had nothing to do with the fight or the death. Twenty-two young men were put on trial. There was no proof that José was killed on purpose. But, 12 young men were found guilty of murder.

Francisca asked to help with the case. She worked with a group that tried to get the facts of the case printed in newspapers and aired on the radio. She wanted people to know how badly the Hispanic Americans had been treated. This work was the start of her job as a writer. For the rest of her life, Francisca wrote articles. She also helped edit magazines that were written in Spanish.

In the 1950s, Francisca worked with unions. These groups helped workers get better jobs. Around that time, a movie was made. It was called *Salt of the Earth*. It told the story of a strike at a mine. The mine was a place where many Hispanic Americans worked. The government made it against the law to watch the film. But, Francisca planned secret meetings. People could come, watch the movie, and learn about the strike.

In the 1960s, Francisca praised Dr. Martin Luther King Jr. for his civil rights work. She told others that they should march with him. In the 1970s, Francisca became the first president of a new group for women's rights. The group ran a center to help Hispanic women learn new skills and find jobs. Francisca was always proud of her Hispanic American background. She wanted her people to be a bridge between the Americas. Her work showed the way.

Francisca Flores
(1913–1996)

1. Which word best describes Francisca Flores?

   a. exhausted

   b. strong

   c. vain

   d. silent

2. What does the word **struggles** mean in the passage?

   a. victories

   b. hard efforts

   c. wounds

   d. investments

3. Number the following events in the order they happened.

   _____ Francisca planned secret showings of *Salt of the Earth*.

   _____ Francisca started a new women's rights group.

   _____ Francisca became ill with TB.

   _____ Francisca learned about Mexican history in the hospital.

   _____ Francisca helped get the facts about the Sleepy Lagoon trial printed in newspapers and aired on the radio.

4. Answer the following questions.

   What was Sleepy Lagoon?

   _____

   _____

   What did Francisca do to help during the Sleepy Lagoon trial?

   _____

   _____

   Where was Francisca born?

   _____

   Whose work did Francisca praise in the 1960s?

   _____

5. Why did Francisca have to plan secret meetings to show *Salt of the Earth*?

   a. The government did not want people to see the movie.

   b. Too many people would come to see it if the meetings were not secret.

   c. The government made it against the law to watch the film.

   d. a and c

Bonus

What is your background? From which country or countries did your family come to this country? Tell how you feel to have the background that you do.

Romana Acosta Banuelos
(1925– _____)

The young Mexican girl was only 16 years old. She had two children to care for, and now her husband had left. But, Romana Banuelos was a strong individual. She knew that she could find a way to support her family.

Romana had a relative who lived in Los Angeles, California, so she moved there. Romana immediately started looking for work. At first, the only job she could find was washing dishes. Then, she got a job making tacos. She worked from midnight until six o'clock in the morning. Every morning, she went home to care for her children.

Romana worked like this until she saved $500. That was enough to buy a tortilla-making machine. Romana had helped her mother make food to sell when she lived in Mexico, and her idea was to start a business like that in the United States. She had a lot to do. She needed to learn English. She needed to make and save more money. She needed to learn all that she could about running a business. Romana always made sure that she was working toward her **goals**.

By 1949, Romana had started her own food company. She named it after her daughter, Ramona. The profits from the business were invested back into the company to help it grow. Within 20 years, Ramona Mexican Food Products was the biggest Mexican food business in the country. The company still sells frozen foods to stores across the country.

In 1964, Romana and some other business people bought a small bank. They wanted to help Hispanic Americans and other minorities get loans. This would make it possible for them to buy homes and start businesses. The bank was named Pan American.

With a food business to run and a bank to manage, Romana was very busy. But in 1971, she received a surprising job offer. The president of the United States, Richard Nixon, asked Romana to be the United States treasurer.

Romana was the first Hispanic American female to become U.S. treasurer. She served in the position for more than two years. During that time, Romana's signature was printed on every piece of paper money made in the United States.

Today, Romana and her daughter run the Pan American Bank together. Her family still owns Ramona Mexican Food Products, too. And, Romana has taught many women by her example that they can set goals and find ways to improve their lives.

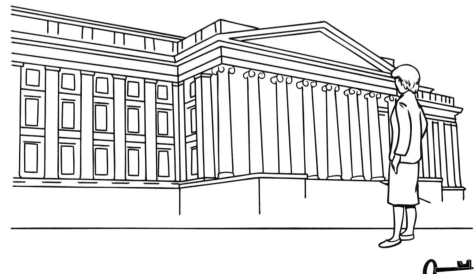

Romana Acosta Banuelos
(1925– _____)

The young Mexican girl was only 16 years old. She had two children to care for. Now, her husband had left. But, Romana Banuelos was very strong. She knew that she could find a way to support her family.

Romana had a relative who lived in Los Angeles, California. She moved there. She looked for work. At first, the only job she could find was washing dishes. Then, she got a job making tacos. She worked from midnight until six o'clock in the morning. She went home every morning to take care of her children.

Romana worked like this until she saved $500. She used the money to buy a tortilla machine. Romana had helped her mother make food to sell when she lived in Mexico. She wanted to start a business like that in the United States. She had a lot to do. She needed to save more money. She needed to learn how to run a business. She needed to learn English. Romana worked hard to meet all of her **goals**.

By 1949, Romana had started her own food company. She named the company after her daughter, Ramona. The money she made was put back into the business to help it grow. Ramona Mexican Food Products became the biggest Mexican food business in the country within 20 years. It still sells frozen foods to stores across the country.

In 1964, Romana and some other business people bought a small bank. They wanted to help Hispanic Americans and others get loans. This would make it possible for them to buy homes. They could start businesses. The bank was named Pan American.

With a food business to run and a bank to manage, Romana was very busy. But in 1971, she got a surprising job offer. The president of the United States, Richard Nixon, asked Romana to be the United States treasurer.

Romana was the first Hispanic American woman to be U.S. treasurer. She served in the position for more than two years. During that time, Romana's signature was printed on every piece of paper money made in the United States.

Today, Romana and her daughter run the Pan American Bank together. Her family still owns Ramona Mexican Food Products. And, Romana has taught many women that they can set goals and find ways to make their lives better.

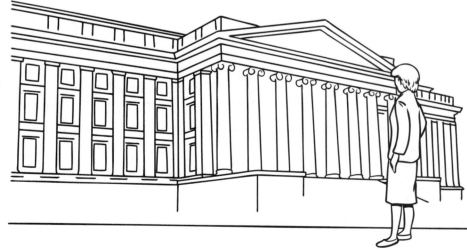

Romana Acosta Banuelos
(1925– ____)

1. The third paragraph is mainly about:

    a. Romana's life in Mexico.

    b. Romana's daughter.

    c. Romana's idea for the business she wanted to start.

    d. Romana's relative in Los Angeles, California.

2. What does the word **goals** mean in the passage?

    a. places to shoot balls or pucks

    b. tight grips

    c. long-term plans

    d. extra scores in sports

3. Number the following events in the order they happened.

    _____ Romana helped start a bank for minorities.

    _____ Romana's husband left.

    _____ Romana started a food business in California.

    _____ Romana became the treasurer of the United States.

    _____ Romana got a job washing dishes.

4. Answer the following questions.

    What did Romana name after her daughter?

    _____

    _____

    Why did Romana save $500?

    _____

    _____

    What help does the Pan American Bank give to people?

    _____

    _____

    Who runs the bank with Romana today?

    _____

5. Which president asked Romana to take the job of U.S. treasurer?

    a. Gerald R. Ford

    b. Lyndon B. Johnson

    c. Dwight D. Eisenhower

    d. none of the above

Bonus
Write about a time when you set a goal for yourself. What happened? Did you meet your goal?

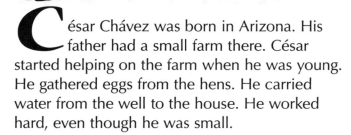

César Estrada Chávez
(1927–1993)

César Chávez was born in Arizona. His father had a small farm there. César started helping on the farm when he was young. He gathered eggs from the hens. He carried water from the well to the house. He worked hard, even though he was small.

César's father worked hard, too. He tried to pay for his farm by clearing 80 acres of land. He was told that when the land was cleared, he would be given 40 acres for his farm. But, the man who made this deal cheated César's father, selling the land to someone else instead. César's father did not have money to buy the land, so César's family lost their home. They became **migrant farm workers**. This meant that they had to move from one farm to another, looking for work. César was 10 years old.

César's parents wanted him to attend school, but it was hard because the family moved often. César and his brother went to 37 different schools. Many of them did not allow César to speak Spanish, and he did not know much English. This made lessons very challenging and difficult.

All of the Chávez children had to do farm work, laboring all day. Sometimes, there was no water to drink and no shade to protect them from the hot sun. Even though the whole family worked, they did not make enough money to live well. But, César's parents gave away food to needier people. Sometimes, César's mother asked him to go to the fields, find a hungry person, and bring that worker home for a meal.

When César grew up, he wanted to help the farm workers, too. First, he worked for a group that helped people register to vote.

Then, César started a union, the United Farm Workers. César wanted farm workers to receive fair pay. He wanted them to have water to drink while they worked, better places to stay at big farms, and bathrooms. The people who owned the farms did not like César, because they did not want to pay to improve conditions for the migrant workers.

César led the workers as they went on strike. This meant that they stopped working. They waited until they won agreements from their employers. César also fasted—he stopped eating. The press reported on his fasts, which drew attention to the strikes. The fasts proved that the workers were dedicated to improving their lives. One time, César fasted for 36 days.

Things started to change for the farm workers. Some owners gave the workers better pay, water to drink, clean places to stay, and bathrooms. César died when he was 66 years old. But, the work went on. In 1994, President Bill Clinton honored César with the Medal of Freedom. Even though César is gone, no one will forget his brave stand for farm workers.

César Estrada Chávez
(1927–1993)

César Chávez was born in Arizona. His father had a small farm there. César started working on the farm when he was small. He took eggs from the hens. He carried water from the well to the house. He worked hard.

César's father worked hard, too. He tried to pay for his farm. He was asked to clear 80 acres of land. Then, he would get 40 acres for his farm. But, the man who made this deal cheated César's father. He sold the land to someone else instead. César's father did not have money to buy the land. So, César's family lost their home. They became **migrant farm workers**. This meant that they had to move from one farm to another, looking for work. César was 10 years old.

César's parents wanted him to go to school. But, this was hard. The family moved a lot. César and his brother went to 37 different schools. Many of them did not let César speak Spanish. He did not know much English. So, lessons were very hard for him.

All of the Chávez children had to do farm work. They worked all day. Sometimes, there was no water to drink. Sometimes, there was no shade to protect them from the hot sun. Even though the whole family worked, they did not make enough money. But, César's parents gave away food to others. Sometimes, César's mother asked him to go to the fields and find a hungry person. She told César to bring that person home for a meal.

When César grew up, he wanted to help farm workers, too. First, he worked for a group that helped people learn how to vote. Then, César started a union for farm workers.

It was called the United Farm Workers. César wanted farm workers to get fair pay. He wanted them to have water to drink while they worked. He wanted them to have better places to stay at big farms where they worked. The people who owned the farms did not like César. They did not want to pay to make things better.

César helped workers go on strike. This meant that they stopped working. They waited until they got the things they needed. César also fasted. This meant that he stopped eating. The press reported on his fasts. This drew attention to the strikes. The fasts showed that the workers would do anything to improve their lives. Once, César fasted for 36 days.

Things started to change for the farm workers. Some owners gave the workers better pay. They made sure that they had water to drink, clean places to stay, and bathrooms. César died when he was 66 years old. But, the work went on. In 1994, President Bill Clinton honored César with the Medal of Freedom. Even though César is gone, no one will forget his brave work.

César Estrada Chávez
(1927–1993)

1. The second paragraph is mainly about:

   a. how César's father lost his farm.

   b. how César started a union.

   c. how César worked on his father's farm.

   d. how César helped the farm workers.

2. What does the term **migrant farm workers** mean in the passage?

   a. workers who own their own farms

   b. the owners of big farms who hire a lot of workers

   c. workers who have to keep moving from one job to the next on different farms

   d. workers who live on their own farms but work somewhere else

3. Number the following events in the order they happened.

   _____ The Chávez family lost their home.

   _____ César fasted for 36 days.

   _____ César helped farm workers learn how to vote.

   _____ President Bill Clinton honored César with the Medal of Freedom.

   _____ César helped with chores on his father's farm.

4. Answer the following questions.

   What problem did César have while going to school?

   _____

   _____

   What is the United Farm Workers?

   _____

   _____

   Where did César live until he was 10 years old?

   _____

   What award was César given after he died?

   _____

5. According to the author, why did César fast?

   a. The fasts showed that the farm workers would do anything to get what they needed.

   b. The fasts drew attention to the strikes.

   c. The press reported on the fasts, so people knew what was happening.

   d. all of the above

Bonus

What would it be like to go to a school and not understand the language that the teacher and students used? How would this make everything harder to learn? Write a paragraph about it.

Lauro Cavazos
(1927– ____)

Lauro Cavazos is from a family with deep roots. His family played a part in the history of Texas. Then, Lauro played a part in history, too—in the history of the United States.

One of the best-known members of Lauro's family was a woman named Francita Alavez. She helped soldiers who were hurt during the Mexican Revolution. That was in the 1830s. Lauro's family has lived in Texas for nearly 200 years.

Lauro's father was one of *Los Kineños*, the King Men. This is the name for the special cowboys who work on the huge King Ranch in Texas. These cowboys are among the best in the world. Lauro's father was a foreman. He helped run the ranch and was a leader of the other cowboys.

The King Ranch is so vast that people can get lost on it. The Cavazos family's house was far away from any town or neighbor. They could not even hear radio broadcasts. But, it was not lonely. Lauro's father wanted his children to learn everything they could, and he made sure that they had a lot of books to read.

Lauro and his two brothers loved their father. But, none of them wanted to be cowboys. They grew up and trained for other jobs. Lauro became a teacher. He taught as a professor at a medical school. Later, in 1980, he was made president of Texas Tech University.

Lauro became an **expert** on teaching, and for this reason, he was given a great honor in 1988. President Ronald Reagan asked Lauro to serve in his cabinet. Lauro became the secretary of education and was in charge of the quality of teaching around the United States. He was the first Hispanic American to serve in this important position.

After Lauro left Washington, D.C., and his government office, he returned to the teaching that he loves. Another occupation that Lauro has is writing. He has written many books and articles about medicine and teaching. In 2006, Lauro wrote his autobiography. Sometimes, Lauro gives speeches about growing up on the King Ranch. When he does that, he gets to go back in time as he recalls his special Texan childhood.

Lauro Cavazos
(1927– ____)

Lauro Cavazos is from a family with deep roots. His family played a part in the history of Texas. Then, Lauro played a part in history, too—in the history of the United States.

One member of Lauro's family was a woman named Francita Alavez. She helped soldiers who were hurt during the Mexican Revolution. That was in the 1830s. Lauro's family has lived in Texas for nearly 200 years.

Lauro's father was one of *Los Kineños*. That means "the King Men." It is the name for the special cowboys who work on the huge King Ranch in Texas. These cowboys are among the best in the world. Lauro's father was a foreman. He helped run the ranch. He was a leader of the other cowboys.

The King Ranch is so big that people can get lost on it. The Cavazos family's house was far away from any town or neighbor. They could not even hear radio broadcasts. But, it was not lonely. Lauro's father wanted his children to learn a lot. He made sure that they had a lot of books to read.

Lauro and his two brothers loved their father. But, none of them wanted to be cowboys. They grew up and trained for other jobs. Lauro became a teacher. He taught at a medical school. Later, in 1980, he was made president of Texas Tech University.

Lauro became an **expert** on teaching. This is why he was given a great honor in 1988. President Ronald Reagan asked Lauro to serve in his cabinet. Lauro became the secretary of education. This meant that Lauro was in charge of the quality of teaching around the country. He was the first Hispanic American to serve in this important position.

After Lauro left his job in Washington, D.C., he went back to the teaching that he loves. Another thing that Lauro does is write. He has written many books and articles about medicine and teaching. In 2006, Lauro wrote his life story. Sometimes, Lauro gives speeches about growing up on the King Ranch. When he does that, he gets to go back in time as he thinks about his special Texan childhood.

Lauro Cavazos
(1927– _____)

1. Choose a good title for this passage.

   a. From the King Ranch to the President's Cabinet

   b. The Son of a Cowboy

   c. Teaching Doctors How to Serve

   d. A Famous Family in Texas

2. What does the word **expert** mean in the passage?

   a. to take goods from one country to another

   b. a person who knows a lot about a subject

   c. a person who has bad judgment

   d. someone who lives in a foreign country

3. Number the following events in the order they happened.

   _____ Lauro wrote his life story.

   _____ Lauro became the secretary of education.

   _____ Lauro became the president of a college.

   _____ Lauro started teaching at a medical school.

   _____ Lauro grew up on the King Ranch.

4. Answer the following questions.

   Who are *Los Kineños?*

   _____

   _____

   What important job was Lauro given at Texas Tech University?

   _____

   Who asked Lauro to become the secretary of education?

   _____

   How long has Lauro's family lived in Texas?

   _____

5. What is another way of saying "Lauro is from a family with deep roots"?

   a. Lauro is from a family of farmers.

   b. Lauro is from a family who has stayed in one place for many years.

   c. Lauro is from a family who knows how to grow things.

   d. none of the above

Bonus

Think about the job that a family member or a family friend has. Would you like to do that job, too? Write a paragraph telling why or why not.

Richard Alonso "Pancho" González
(1928–1995)

The crowd was stunned. The tennis match was between a strong, young player and a man who was retired. At age 41, Pancho González was old for a tennis player, even though he was a renowned champion. But, nobody thought that he could play through the longest match in tennis history. Pancho played Charlie Pasarell for 5 hours and 12 minutes. The event took place at Wimbledon in London, England, in 1969. It took two days to finish the match.

Pancho not only lasted through the **brutal** match, but he also won. In one way, Pancho's triumph was not a surprise. There are still many people who think that Pancho was the greatest tennis player who ever lived.

He did not have a promising start in the sport. When he was 12 years old, Pancho wanted a bike for his birthday. His mother would not buy him one. Instead, she bought him a tennis racket for 51 cents. Pancho would take his racket to the tennis courts near his house, sit, and watch the players. Those were the only tennis "lessons" he ever received.

Pancho started missing school to practice tennis. Later, he joined the navy. When he got out, he was 19 years old and was ready to play tennis full-time. Pancho was tall and graceful, and he moved like a big cat. No matter where the tennis ball went, Pancho could launch himself in that direction.

In both 1948 and 1949, Pancho won the U.S. Championship. But, when he was recruited to play professional tennis, he did not do well. In 1951, disappointed, he quit the tour. He bought a tennis shop and played mostly in local games.

Then, in 1952, he played five professional games and won four of them. He kept practicing and improving. In 1954, he journeyed to Australia. He won that tour and beat all of the champions. By the end of that year, Pancho was the top-ranked player in the world.

Pancho stayed at the top of the rankings for the next eight years. No one has ever matched this long string of wins. He persisted even though he faced a lot of prejudice. For example, people said that a scar on his face was from a knife fight. In fact, Pancho had hurt himself while playing on a scooter when he was seven years old. And, even though he was the top-ranked player, he got paid much less than other players on the tour. In 1955, Pancho made $15,000. Another player on the tour, who was white, had an $80,000 contract.

Pancho continued to work as a tennis player and instructor after he stopped touring. He had a fiery temper and did not have many friends. But, even people who did not like him admired his playing. This Hispanic American player made tennis history with his great skill in sports.

Richard Alonso "Pancho" González
(1928–1995)

The crowd was amazed. The tennis match was between a strong, young player and a man who was retired. At age 41, Pancho González was old for a tennis player, even though he was a great one. But, nobody thought that he could last through the longest match in tennis history. Pancho played against Charlie Pasarell for 5 hours and 12 minutes. The game took place at Wimbledon in London, England, in 1969. It took two days to finish the match.

Pancho not only lasted through the **brutal** match, but he also won. In one way, Pancho's win was not a surprise. There are still many people who think that Pancho was the greatest tennis player who ever lived.

He did not have the best start in the sport. When he was 12 years old, Pancho wanted a bike for his birthday. His mother would not buy him one. Instead, she got him a tennis racket. It cost 51 cents. Pancho would take his racket to the tennis courts near his house. He sat and watched the players. Those were the only tennis "lessons" he had.

Pancho started missing school to practice tennis. Later, he joined the navy. When he got out, he was 19 years old. He was ready to play tennis full-time. Pancho was tall. He moved like a big cat. No matter where the tennis ball went, Pancho could move the right way to hit it.

In both 1948 and 1949, Pancho won the U.S. Championship. But, when he was signed to play professional tennis, he did not do well. In 1951, he quit the tour. He bought a tennis shop. He played mostly in local games.

Then, in 1952, he played five professional games and won four of them. He kept playing and kept getting better. In 1954, he went to Australia. He won the tour. He beat all of the champions. By the end of the year, Pancho was the top player in the world.

Pancho stayed on top for the next eight years. No one has ever matched his long string of wins. He kept playing even though he faced a lot of prejudice. For example, people said that a scar on his face was from a knife fight. In fact, Pancho had hurt himself while playing on a scooter when he was seven years old. And, even though he was the top-ranked player, he got paid much less than other players on the tour. In 1955, Pancho made $15,000. Another player on the tour, who was white, had an $80,000 contract.

Pancho kept playing tennis and giving tennis lessons after he stopped touring. He had a bad temper. He did not have many friends. But, even people who did not like him admired his playing. This Hispanic American player made tennis history with his great skill in sports.

Richard Alonso "Pancho" González
(1928–1995)

1. The sixth paragraph of the passage is mainly about:

   a. Pancho's time in the navy.

   b. how Pancho learned to play tennis.

   c. how Pancho came back after leaving tennis and became a champion again.

   d. how Pancho won a famous game of tennis at Wimbledon.

2. What does the word **brutal** mean in the passage?

   a. quiet and easy

   b. light and happy

   c. harsh and tiring

   d. slow and boring

3. Number the following events in the order they happened.

   _____ Pancho dropped out of the professional tour after doing poorly.

   _____ Pancho went to the tennis courts near his home to watch the players.

   _____ Pancho won the longest match in tennis history.

   _____ Pancho stopped touring and worked as a tennis player and instructor.

   _____ Pancho became the top-ranked tennis player in the world.

4. Answer the following questions.

   Who gave Pancho his first tennis racket?

   _____

   In what country did Pancho win a championship in 1954?

   _____

   How long was the longest match in tennis history?

   _____

   What is one detail in the story that shows prejudice against Pancho?

   _____

   _____

5. Which of the following was probably not a help to Pancho in his career?

   a. his early interest in tennis

   b. his height and speed on the court

   c. his bad temper

   d. the way he kept working to make his game better

Bonus

Write a description of a sporting event that you went to. What was the game like? How did the crowd act? Did you enjoy yourself?

Jaime Escalante
(1930– _____)

When Jaime Escalante came to the United States, he had already been a teacher for 14 years. He had taught math and physics in Bolivia, his native country, but he did not speak English. He did not have papers that said that he could teach in the state of California. This meant that he had a lot of hard work to do.

Fortunately, Jaime was never afraid of hard work. He went to night school after working all day at a computer company. He learned English, and he earned a math degree from an American college. This allowed him to get a teaching job.

The school where Jaime found a job was in East Los Angeles, California. The city was known for its gangs, drugs, and violence. At first, Jaime was not sure that he could teach there, but then, he found a small group of students who really wanted to learn higher math. In 1982, 18 of his students passed the Advanced Placement (AP) exam in calculus, thanks to Jaime's gifted teaching and their hard work.

The students were thrilled. But, their happiness did not last long. The testing service that graded the papers took back the scores. They said that the students must have cheated, because students from that school could never have earned such high scores. Jaime talked almost all of the students into taking the test a second time. They all passed again. This time, the story was aired on TV and printed in newspapers.

People around the country learned about Jaime's teaching and the way he refused to give up on his students. But, the best outcome was that more students wanted to be in Jaime's classes. In 1987, the number of students at the school taking the AP exam grew to 85. Out of those students, 73 passed the regular AP exam, and the other 12 passed an even harder **version** of the test.

In 1988, a movie was made about Jaime and his students. It was called *Stand and Deliver*. It told the story of how Jaime got his students interested in math, and it created even more interest in Jaime's teaching methods. Many well-known people wanted to visit his class and watch him teach. Even President George H. W. Bush came to meet him. Jaime was awarded the Presidential Medal for Excellence in Education in 1988.

In 1991, Jaime left the school in East Los Angeles because of disagreements with a new principal. He went to teach in Sacramento, California. After that, he hosted a TV show that showed students how they could use their studies to find many different types of jobs. In 1998, he was given a medal by the Organization of American States.

Jaime Escalante
(1930– _____)

Jaime Escalante had already been a teacher for 14 years when he came to the United States. He had taught in Bolivia, his native land. But, he did not speak English. He did not have papers that said he could teach in California. This meant that he had a lot of hard work to do.

But, Jaime was never afraid of hard work. He worked all day at a computer company. Then, he went to night school. He learned English. And, he got a math degree from an American college. This let him get a teaching job.

The job was at a school in East Los Angeles, California. The city was known for its gangs, drugs, and violence. At first, Jaime was not sure that he could teach there. Then, he found a small group of students who really wanted to learn math. In 1982, 18 of his students passed an Advanced Placement (AP) calculus exam, thanks to Jaime's teaching and their hard work.

The students were excited. But, the testing service that graded their papers took back the scores. They said that the students must have cheated. They said that no students from their school could have gotten such high scores. Jaime got almost all of the students to take the test again. They all passed a second time. This time, the story was aired on TV. It was printed in newspapers.

People around the country heard about Jaime's teaching. They read about how he stood by his students. But even better, more students at the school wanted to take math.

They wanted to be in Jaime's classes. In 1987, 85 students at the school took the AP test. All of them passed it. Twelve of them even passed a harder **version** of the test.

In 1988, a movie called *Stand and Deliver* was released. It was about Jaime and his students. The movie told how Jaime got his students interested in math. Even more people found out about Jaime's teaching style. Many well-known people wanted to visit his class and watch Jaime teach. Even President George H. W. Bush came to meet him. Jaime was given the Presidential Medal for Excellence in Education in 1988.

In 1991, Jaime left his school. A new principal had come to the school. Jaime did not agree with the principal's way of doing things. He went to teach in Sacramento, California. Later, he hosted a TV show. It showed students how to use their studies to find many different kinds of jobs. In 1998, he was given a medal by the Organization of American States.

Jaime Escalante
(1930– _____)

1. This passage tells about:

   a. growing up in Bolivia.

   b. a man who wanted to be a teacher but was never able to teach.

   c. a teacher who taught higher math to students in a dangerous city.

   d. a student who met President George H. W. Bush.

2. What does the word **version** mean in the passage?

   a. something that varies from the original

   b. something that is green and lush

   c. something that rhymes

   d. something that is exactly the same as another

3. Number the following events in the order they happened.

   _____ Jaime went to night school.

   _____ Jaime was given the Presidential Medal for Excellence in Education.

   _____ Jaime came to the United States.

   _____ Jaime left East Los Angeles to teach in Sacramento, California.

   _____ Eighteen of Jaime's students passed the AP calculus exam.

4. Answer the following questions.

   Why didn't Jaime start teaching right away in the United States?

   _____

   _____

   What was the name of the movie made about Jaime and his students?

   _____

   What subject did Jaime teach?

   _____

   What was the topic of the TV show that Jaime hosted?

   _____

   _____

5. Why might the testing company have thought that Jaime's students cheated?

   a. The students were from a school that had never had high scores before.

   b. The students were from a dangerous neighborhood, and the testing company was prejudiced.

   c. The students all passed, and that kind of excellence is unusual in any school.

   d. all of the above

Bonus

Write a short newspaper story about the students retaking the AP exam. Tell how they all passed again. Why did they have to retake the test? What did the second scores prove?

Rita Moreno
(1931– _____)

There are four important awards for performers in the United States. One is the Oscar®, for work in movies. One is the Emmy®, for work on TV. One is the Tony®, for work in stage plays. And, the fourth is the Grammy®, for work in music.

There are only three women who have won all four of these impressive awards, and only one Hispanic American woman has done this. That woman is Rita Moreno.

But, Rita's work as an actor, dancer, and singer did not always look promising. Rita was born to a family of impoverished farmers in Puerto Rico. She came with her mother to the United States for a better life. Rita was five years old when she came to New York City, New York. Right away, it was evident that Rita had talent for theater work. She danced in a show when she was 7 years old, her first acting part onstage came when she was 13, and she earned a part in her first film when she was only 17 years old.

But for the next 10 years, Rita's parts were not substantial ones. She played Hispanic women, American Indians, and a slave princess in Thailand. She once said that in every part, she was barefoot. Because of her race, she was not given starring parts or challenging roles. This showed **prejudice** in the way she was selected for her parts.

That changed in 1961 when Rita got a part in *West Side Story*. It was a very important movie, in which Rita played a girl from Puerto Rico. She acted, sang, and danced in her part. The film's story, based on the play *Romeo and Juliet*, presented a strong message against prejudice. Rita won an Oscar® for her role, which placed her work in the spotlight.

Rita continued acting on the Broadway stage. She was given many excellent parts in plays. She also kept working in films. Rita married a doctor named Lenny Gordon in 1965. He helped manage her career.

In the 1970s, Rita tried something new: TV. She starred in a show for children called *The Electric Company*. She won one of her Grammy® Awards for a recording of her singing in this show. She also acted in *The Muppet Show* with the popular Muppets. Rita chose these parts because she had a young daughter. She wanted her daughter and other children to see a Puerto Rican in the shows that they watched and enjoyed. She continues to perform on TV today.

With her work, Rita helps other Hispanic performers. She was able to break away from the small, demeaning parts she got at the start of her career. She has been told by other actors that she shows them what is possible to achieve, regardless of race.

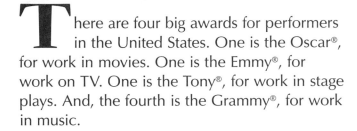
There are four big awards for performers in the United States. One is the Oscar®, for work in movies. One is the Emmy®, for work on TV. One is the Tony®, for work in stage plays. And, the fourth is the Grammy®, for work in music.

There are only three women who have won all four of these big awards. Only one Hispanic American woman has done this. That woman is Rita Moreno.

But, Rita's work as an actor, dancer, and singer did not always look promising. Rita was born to a family of poor farmers. She and her mother came to the United States from Puerto Rico. Rita was five years old when she came to New York City, New York. Right away, it was clear that Rita was good on the stage. She danced in a show when she was 7 years old. Her first acting part onstage came when she was 13. And, Rita was given a part in her first film when she was only 17 years old.

But for the next 10 years, Rita's parts were not good ones. She played Hispanic women, American Indians, and a slave princess in Thailand. She once said that in every part, she was barefoot. Because of her race, she was not given big parts or interesting roles. This showed **prejudice** in the way she was picked for her parts.

That changed in 1961 when Rita got a part in *West Side Story*. It was a very important movie. Rita played a girl from Puerto Rico. She acted, sang, and danced in the part. The movie's story, based on the play *Romeo and Juliet*, spoke against prejudice. Rita won an Oscar® for her role.

Rita returned to acting on the stage. She was given many good parts in plays. She also kept working in movies. Rita got married in 1965. She married a doctor named Lenny Gordon. He helped manage her career.

In the 1970s, Rita tried something new: TV. She starred in a show for kids called *The Electric Company*. She won one of her Grammy® Awards for a recording of her singing in this show. She also acted in *The Muppet Show* with the Muppets. Rita chose these parts because she had a young daughter. She wanted her daughter and other children to see someone from Puerto Rico in the shows that they watched and liked. She continues to act on TV today.

With her work, Rita helps other Hispanic performers. She broke away from the small, bad parts she got at the start of her work life. She has been told by other actors that she helps show them what is possible.

Rita Moreno
(1931– _____)

1. The fourth paragraph is mainly about:

    a. Rita's birth and childhood.

    b. Rita's marriage.

    c. Rita's early career and bad parts.

    d. Rita's awards.

2. What does the word **prejudice** mean in the passage?

    a. hatred of a group that is felt without good reason

    b. the first opinion of a judge

    c. to win a court case

    d. to lose the ability to win

3. Number the following events in the order they happened.

    _____ Rita played a slave princess from Thailand.

    _____ Rita won the Oscar® for her part in *West Side Story*.

    _____ Rita married a doctor who helped with her career.

    _____ Rita had her first part in a play.

    _____ Rita acted in *The Electric Company*.

4. Answer the following questions.

    What is a Tony® Award for?

    _____

    _____

    Where was Rita born?

    _____

    Why did Rita choose to be on *The Muppet Show*?

    _____

    _____

    Why do other actors say that Rita's life has inspired them?

    _____

    _____

5. Which of these talents does Rita have?

    a. She can act.

    b. She can sing.

    c. She can dance.

    d. all of the above

Bonus

Imagine that you are given a part on your favorite TV show. Which character would you want to play? Why?

Cruz Reynoso
(1931– ____)

Cruz Reynoso knows what it means to be poor. His father was a farm worker in California. Cruz grew up in a family of 11 children. He picked grapes and plums with the rest of his family. Every year, he had to start school late. He could not start the year's classes until the farm work was done.

But, Cruz learned good lessons from his early life. When he was 10 years old, he saw the power of people working as a team. The farm workers found out that they were paid much less than workers at the farm next door. They held a strike. They worked with the farm owner to get fair pay. Cruz never forgot this event.

Cruz was not allowed to go to school with white people. People told him that he would never get into college because he was Hispanic American. He did not listen to them. Cruz earned a college degree in 1953. Then, he joined the army for two years. When Cruz got out of the army, he went to law school.

Cruz wanted to do something to help people like those he grew up with. He worked for a group that gave legal advice and help to farm workers. This was one of the first groups to give free legal help to people who could not afford to pay for it. Cruz became the director of the group. His work won attention around the country.

In 1976, Cruz became a judge. Then, in 1982, he was appointed to the supreme court of California. This is the highest court in the state. Cruz was the first Hispanic American to serve on the state supreme court. He held this job for five years. While he was on the court, Cruz heard many civil rights cases. He also **overturned** the death penalty on many cases that came to the court.

In 1991, Cruz decided to become a teacher. He taught law students at two universities in California. He also still teaches about and studies civil rights today. For his work, President Bill Clinton gave Cruz the Medal of Freedom in 2000.

Cruz still writes and speaks about the lives of farm workers. In California, a farm worker's family still makes only about one-sixth of what the average family in California makes each year. In some cases, farm workers are paid even less than they were years ago. Cruz's speeches raise awareness of the many challenges that farm workers face.

Cruz Reynoso
(1931– ____)

Cruz Reynoso knows what it means to be poor. His father was a farm worker in California. Cruz grew up in a family of 11 children. He picked grapes and plums as a child. Every year, he had to start school late. He could not start the year's classes until the farm work was done. Every member of his family had to work.

But, Cruz learned some good lessons from his early life. When he was 10 years old, he saw the power of people working as a team. The farm workers found out that they were paid much less than workers at the farm next door. They held a strike. They worked with the farm owner to get fair pay. Cruz never forgot this event.

Cruz could not go to school with white people. People said that he would never get into college. They said that because he was Hispanic American, he would be turned away. Cruz did not listen to them. He earned a college degree in 1953. Then, he joined the army for two years. When Cruz got out of the army, he went to law school.

Cruz wanted to do something to help people like those he grew up with. He worked for a group that helped farm workers. The group gave workers advice about the law. The farm workers did not have to pay for the help. Cruz was put in charge of the group. People around the country heard about his good work.

In 1976, Cruz became a judge. Then, in 1982, he was appointed to the supreme court of California. This is the highest court in the state. Cruz was the first Hispanic American to serve on the state supreme court. He held this job

for five years. While he was on the court, Cruz heard many civil rights cases. He also **overturned** the death penalty on many cases that came to the court.

In 1991, Cruz became a teacher. He taught at two schools. He still teaches law students. He also teaches about and studies civil rights. To honor his work, President Bill Clinton gave Cruz the Medal of Freedom in 2000.

Cruz still writes and speaks about the lives of farm workers. Most of these families are very poor. Some farm workers are paid even less than they were years ago. Cruz's speeches help people see the problems that farm workers still face.

Cruz Reynoso
(1931– ____)

1. The third paragraph is mostly about:

   a. how Cruz helped his family.

   b. how Cruz went to college.

   c. how Cruz became a judge.

   d. how Cruz became a teacher.

2. What does the word **overturned** mean in the passage?

   a. destroyed

   b. defeated

   c. put back to the way it was to begin with

   d. bent

3. Number the following events in the order they happened.

   _____ Cruz was born to a large family of farm workers.

   _____ Cruz joined a group that helped farm workers by giving them advice about the law.

   _____ Cruz became a judge on the supreme court of California.

   _____ Cruz was given the Medal of Freedom.

   _____ Cruz went to college.

4. Answer the following questions.

Why did Cruz have to start school late every year?

_____

_____

Which president honored Cruz's work?

_____

In what year did Cruz become a judge?

_____

What is one subject that Cruz studies and teaches about?

_____

5. Why was the strike Cruz saw when he was 10 years old so important to him?

   a. The farm workers fought for their rights together and won.

   b. The farm owners showed how powerful they were.

   c. The farm workers were not able to get what they wanted.

   d. He knew that he had no power to stand up to the farm owners.

Bonus

If you could do one thing to help farm workers today, what would it be? Write about it. Be sure to explain why you chose that kind of help.

Roberto Clemente never looked completely comfortable when he was at bat. He stretched his neck and his back. But, he could hit the ball well. And, when he ran, he was incredible. His legs and arms pumped so hard that his helmet would fly off his head.

It was in the field, though, where Roberto really shone. He always seemed to know exactly where the ball was going. He had a powerful throwing arm. One joke about Roberto was that he could field a game in one state and throw out a player in another state at the same time.

Roberto grew up in Puerto Rico. When Roberto was in high school, he was good at track. He won medals for his short races. But, baseball was the game he loved best. When he was 17 years old, Roberto joined a Puerto Rican baseball team, where his batting, fielding, and strong throwing arm earned a lot of attention.

Roberto signed with the Brooklyn Dodgers in 1953. He said later that the team had not treated him fairly. He was sent to the minors in Montreal, Canada, where he was put on the bench if he did well. If he was doing badly, they made him keep playing. Roberto was glad to be drafted by the Pittsburgh Pirates in 1955. That is when he really got to start playing.

With every passing year, it became clearer what a great player Roberto was. He won four batting crowns, and he was given the Gold Glove award for fielding 12 times in a row. He was on the World Series team in 1960—the first time that the Pirates had made it to the Series in 33 years. He was on the Pirates World Series team again in 1971.

But, Roberto won only one Most Valuable Player (MVP) Award. Other baseball players won more honors and titles than he did. He felt that this was because of his race.

In Puerto Rico and other Hispanic countries, though, Roberto was a hero. At the end of 1972, there was a catastrophic earthquake in Nicaragua. Roberto helped gather food and supplies for the people there. On New Year's Eve, he took off in a plane with these supplies, but the plane crashed in the sea. Roberto died at the age of 38.

It usually takes five years after the end of a player's career for him to be eligible to be voted into the Baseball Hall of Fame. But, the Hall of Fame voted to put Roberto in right away. He was the first Hispanic American to be honored in this way. There was another honor given to Roberto that he might have liked even better: in Puerto Rico, a baseball **stadium** is named after him.

Roberto Clemente
(1934–1972)

Roberto Clemente never looked relaxed when he was at bat. He stretched his neck. He stretched his back. But, he could hit the ball well. And, when he ran, he was amazing. His legs and arms pumped so hard that his helmet would fly off his head.

In the field, Roberto really shone. He always seemed to know where the ball was going. He had a strong throwing arm. One joke about Roberto was that he could field a game in one state and throw out a player in another state at the same time.

Roberto grew up in Puerto Rico. When Roberto was in high school, he was good at track. He won medals for short races. But, baseball was the game he loved best. When he was 17 years old, Roberto joined a Puerto Rican baseball team. His batting, fielding, and strong throwing arm earned a lot of attention.

Roberto signed with the Brooklyn Dodgers in 1953. He said later that the team had not treated him fairly. He was sent to the minors in Montreal, Canada. He was put on the bench if he did well. If he did badly, they made him keep playing. Roberto was glad to be drafted by the Pittsburgh Pirates in 1955. That is when he really got to start playing.

It became clearer every year that Roberto was a great player. He won four batting crowns. He won the Gold Glove award for fielding 12 times in a row. He was on two World Series teams with the Pirates. One was in 1960, and the other was in 1971.

But, Roberto won only one Most Valuable Player (MVP) Award. Other baseball players won more honors than he did. He felt that this was because of his race.

In Puerto Rico and other Hispanic countries, though, Roberto was a hero. At the end of 1972, there was a big earthquake in Nicaragua. Roberto helped collect food and supplies for the people there. On New Year's Eve, he took off in a plane with these supplies. But, the plane crashed in the sea. Roberto died. He was only 38 years old.

The Baseball Hall of Fame usually does not vote in players until five years after their careers end. But, in this case, the Hall of Fame did not wait. In 1973, Roberto was voted into the Hall of Fame. He was the first Hispanic American to be given this honor. In Puerto Rico, he was given another honor that he might have liked even more. A baseball **stadium** is named after him.

Roberto Clemente
(1934–1972)

1. Choose a good title for this passage.

   a. Baseball in the 1950s and 1960s

   b. A Baseball Legend

   c. Baseball in Puerto Rico

   d. The Greatest Batter in the World

2. What does the word **stadium** mean in the passage?

   a. a state or region

   b. a quiet place with trees and walks

   c. a place to play outdoor sports, with a field and seats

   d. a place to park cars, with many stories of parking places

3. Number the following events in the order they happened.

   _____ Roberto was drafted by the Pittsburgh Pirates.

   _____ Roberto ran track in high school.

   _____ Roberto planned to take supplies to earthquake victims.

   _____ Roberto played baseball on a team in Puerto Rico.

   _____ Roberto won an MVP award.

4. Answer the following questions.

   What team from the United States drafted Roberto first?

   _____

   In what years did Roberto play in the World Series?

   _____

   In what country was there a big earthquake in 1972?

   _____

   How many times did Roberto win a Gold Glove award for fielding?

   _____

5. Why did Roberto feel that he did not get as many awards as other players?

   a. He felt that it was because he was Hispanic American.

   b. He felt that it was because of his strange batting style.

   c. He felt that it was because of his bad playing.

   d. none of the above

Bonus

Write a poem about baseball. You might write about playing the sport, about watching a game, or about your favorite player.

Richard Serra
(1939– _____)

Richard Serra was born in San Francisco, California. Although he has not lived there for many years, he still thinks of himself as a Californian. His family was not wealthy, but they had a good time and enjoyed each other's company.

Richard's father was born in Spain. He worked in a jelly bean factory. Richard's mother was from Russia. She taught her children that there was little value in material things. She said that it was better to spend time reflecting and having interesting experiences in life. Richard attended college in California. He also spent a lot of time on Rosarita Beach, where he studied and surfed. He had a job at a steel mill, which helped him pay for school.

One of Richard's favorite teachers was his art teacher. He convinced Richard to go to Mexico to see some huge wall paintings, or murals, that were being painted there at the time. Richard loved the paintings.

Then, Richard got to attend Yale University. He had sent 12 drawings to the art school there, and he was given a scholarship. Richard studied painting. The school even gave him enough money to travel to Paris, France, and Florence, Italy. Just as he did in Mexico, Richard went to these places to look at art there.

Richard started creating **sculptures** in 1966. His first pieces were not large. But, Richard loved working with steel. The time he had spent at the steel mill worked its way into his art. Today, he is best known for his huge steel sculptures.

For a museum in Spain, Richard made some of these enormous steel sculptures. The steel came in rolls that were 50 feet long. The curving walls of one sculpture are 14 feet high. The steel used to make each of the sculpture's walls had to be so large and thick that there was only one steel mill in the world that could manufacture it.

Some people love Richard's art, finding his large pieces calm and solid. But, other people do not like his work. Richard's art made headlines in 1989. A sculpture he made, called *Tilted Arc,* was taken down in New York City. It was a huge, curved wall of rusted steel. Office workers in a building nearby wanted it torn down, because it cut their plaza in half. Richard said that that was the point. They had to look at the sculpture while they walked around it. But, the workers won, and the piece was cut apart and hauled away.

Richard still makes his gigantic steel sculptures. His art still angers some people, but many others think that he is one of the greatest artists in the world today.

Richard Serra was born in San Francisco, California. He has not lived there for many years. But, he still thinks of himself as a person from California. His family was not rich, but they had a good time together.

Richard's father was from Spain. He worked in a jelly bean factory. Richard's mother was from Russia. She taught her children that there was little value in material things. It was better to spend time thinking and doing interesting things. Richard went to college in California. He spent a lot of time on Rosarita Beach, where he studied and surfed. He also had a job at a steel mill. This job helped him pay for school.

One of Richard's favorite teachers was his art teacher. He told Richard to go to Mexico. Richard traveled there to see some huge wall paintings, or murals, that were being painted there at the time. Richard loved the paintings.

Then, Richard got to go to Yale University. He had sent 12 drawings to the art school. Yale gave him money to go to school there. Richard studied painting. The school even gave him money to go to Paris, France, and Florence, Italy. Just like in Mexico, Richard went to these places to look at the art there.

Richard started making **sculptures** in 1966. His first pieces were not large. But, Richard loved working with steel. The time he had spent at the steel mill worked its way into his art. Today, he is known best for his huge steel sculptures.

For a museum in Spain, Richard made some of these big steel sculptures. The steel came in rolls that were 50 feet long. The curving walls of one sculpture are 14 feet high. The steel used to make each of the sculpture's walls had to be very large and thick. There was only one steel mill in the world that could make it.

Some people love Richard's art. They find his big pieces to be calm and solid. But, other people do not like his work. Richard's art made headlines in 1989. A big piece in New York City was taken down. It was called *Tilted Arc*. It was a huge, curved wall of rusted steel. Office workers in a building nearby wanted it taken down. They said that it cut their plaza in half. Richard said that that was the point. They had to look at the sculpture while they walked around it. But, the workers won. The piece was cut apart and taken away.

Richard still makes his giant steel sculptures. His art still angers some people. But, many others think that he is one of the greatest artists in the world today.

Richard Serra
(1939– _____)

1. The second paragraph is mainly about:

   a. Richard's sculptures.

   b. Richard's time at Yale University.

   c. Richard's family and youth.

   d. Richard's time in Europe.

2. What does the word **sculptures** mean in the passage?

   a. huge paintings done on walls

   b. artists

   c. big pieces of steel that can be used to make art

   d. works of three-dimensional art shaped using different materials

3. Number the following events in the order they happened.

   _____ Richard went to art school at Yale University.

   _____ Richard was born in San Francisco, California.

   _____ Richard went to college in California.

   _____ One of Richard's sculptures was taken down in 1989.

   _____ Richard traveled to Paris, France, and Florence, Italy.

4. Answer the following questions.

   What did Richard's mother feel was more important than material things?

   _____

   _____

   What was *Tilted Arc*?

   _____

   _____

   Where did Richard learn to work with steel?

   _____

   What did Richard's father do for a living?

   _____

5. What does it mean for something to "make headlines"?

   a. It is written about in newspapers and talked about in news reports.

   b. It is something made out of newspapers and glue.

   c. It is a small story that does not get a lot of attention in the press.

   d. It is something that happens so fast that people do not know about it.

Bonus
If you were going to make sculptures, what would they be like? What materials would you use? What titles would you give the sculptures?

Miguel Algarin
(1941– ____)

Miguel Algarin was born in Puerto Rico, but he immigrated to the United States with his family when he was a small child. His parents loved the arts. Miguel did, too. He started to read the plays and poetry of William Shakespeare, and these writings became very important to him.

Miguel thought about how Shakespeare had a place where he could tell his stories: the Globe Theater. Miguel dreamed of a time when he could have a place to tell stories, too. He wanted to tell stories about New York City, especially the part of the city called the Lower East Side.

When Miguel grew up, he made this dream come true. He finished school and became a college English professor. He taught Shakespeare, and he also taught creative writing. But, his teaching was only a portion of his life.

In 1973, Miguel had an apartment in New York City. Every weekend, he invited poets and writers to come over. They read their work aloud to each other. Miguel wrote stories and poems about New York's Lower East Side. It was what he had always wanted to do.

The apartment became too small for all of the writers and artists who wanted to share their work. Miguel knew that he needed a bigger place. He wanted a place like the Globe Theater, where many people could come to enjoy the arts. In 1975, he found a **café** called The Sunshine Café. He and his friends rented

it and gave it a new name. It is now called the Nuyorican Poets Café. *Nuyorican* is a word that describes Puerto Ricans in New York City.

The café was a huge success. Miguel had to expand it in 1980 by buying another building for additional space. Today, arts activities are held there every day. Poets and writers read their work. Artists display pictures on the walls. People put on plays. Bands come to perform their music.

Miguel retired from teaching, but he still runs the café and is the producer of the theater there. He even hosts a radio show once a week that showcases the people who perform at the café and their art. The plays and music launched from the café have won many awards. Miguel's writing has, too—he won six American Book Awards. Just like Shakespeare, Miguel has done a great deal to bring his stories to people who love to hear them.

Miguel Algarin was born in Puerto Rico. But, he came to the United States as a small child. His parents loved the arts. Miguel did, too. He started to read the plays and poetry of William Shakespeare. This writing became very important to him.

Miguel thought about how Shakespeare had a place where he could tell his stories. It was a theater called the Globe Theater. Miguel dreamed of a time when he could have a place to tell stories, too. He wanted to tell stories about New York City. He wanted to write about a part of the city called the Lower East Side.

When Miguel grew up, he made this dream come true. He finished school. Then, he got a job teaching English at a college. He taught students about Shakespeare. He also taught writing. But, that was only part of his life.

In 1973, Miguel had an apartment in New York City. Every weekend, he asked poets and writers to come over. They read their work aloud. Miguel wrote stories and poems, too. He wrote about New York's Lower East Side. It was what he had always wanted to do.

The apartment became too small for all of the writers and artists who wanted to share their work. Miguel knew that he needed a bigger place. He wanted a place like the Globe Theater, where many people could come to enjoy the arts. In 1975, he found an empty **café** called The Sunshine Café. He and his friends rented it. They gave it a new name. It is now called

the Nuyorican Poets Café. *Nuyorican* is a word that describes Puerto Ricans in New York City.

The café was a big hit. Miguel had to make it bigger in 1980. He bought another building for extra space. Today, arts activities are held there every day. Poets and writers come to read their work. Artists hang pictures on the walls. People put on plays. Bands come to play their music.

Miguel retired from teaching. But, he still runs the café. He is in charge of the theater there. He even puts on a radio show once a week. It is about all of the people from the café and their work. The plays and music from the café have won many awards. Miguel's writing has, too. He has won six American Book Awards. Just like Shakespeare, Miguel has done a lot to bring his stories to people who love to hear them.

Miguel Algarin
(1941– _____)

1. The first paragraph is mainly about:

    a. the books that Miguel has written.

    b. Miguel's childhood.

    c. Miguel's teaching job.

    d. what Miguel does today.

2. What does the word **café** mean in the passage?

    a. a place that rents DVDs

    b. a place where people drink coffee, talk, and see arts events

    c. a type of park

    d. a movie theater

3. Number the following events in the order they happened.

    _____ Miguel started teaching college students.

    _____ Miguel bought another building to give the café more space.

    _____ Miguel moved with his family to New York City.

    _____ Miguel and his friends turned an empty café into a place for art and music.

    _____ Miguel retired from teaching.

4. Answer the following questions.

    Where was Miguel born?

    _____

    What writer inspired Miguel to tell stories?

    _____

    When did Miguel start asking artists and poets to come to his apartment?

    _____

    What is one kind of event that happens at the Nuyorican Poets Café?

    _____

    _____

5. What does the author say was Miguel's dream?

    a. He wanted to write stories and have a place to share them.

    b. He wanted to be the leader of a band.

    c. He wanted to teach students about history.

    d. He wanted to go back to the place where he was born.

Bonus

Would you rather be a poet, an actor, a member of a band, or a dancer? Choose one. Then, write a paragraph explaining your choice.

Ritchie Valens
(1941–1959)

Ritchie Valens's time in the spotlight was brief, lasting only eight months. But, the music of this gifted singer-songwriter is still loved by many.

Born Ricardo Steven Valenzuela, Ritchie grew up in a Mexican American neighborhood in California. He heard a lot of Mexican music during his childhood, and he loved it. But, he also liked other music, especially the blues and rock and roll.

By the time Ritchie was five years old, he wanted to play music of his own. His father, a music lover, encouraged him. Ritchie obtained an old guitar. He was left-handed, and the guitar was made for right-handed players. But, Ritchie was so determined to play that he taught himself how to use the guitar anyway. Ritchie also taught himself how to play the drums, and he started to write his own **lyrics**. But, Ritchie was quiet and shy, and he did not like to show off. Did he have the personality of a musician who could perform in front of people?

When Ritchie was 16 years old, he joined a band that played at dances and parties. When the band's lead singer quit, Ritchie took his place, which helped him feel less shy in front of audiences.

The next year, 1958, was a pivotal year for Ritchie. A record producer named Bob Keane came to hear him play and asked Ritchie to make a record. By September, Ritchie's songs were broadcast around the country. One song, called "Donna," was about a girl Ritchie liked, and it was an instant hit. But, a different song Ritchie sang is the one remembered best today. Ritchie's cousin taught him a Mexican song called "La Bamba." This fiesta song was played at weddings and dances. Musicians wrote their own lyrics for the tune, but some of the words were traditional and stayed the same. Ritchie added a new beat to the music and created a joyful, fast, fun song. Ritchie sang the song in Spanish, which was unusual at the time for an American recording.

Ritchie went on tour. He played in concerts with another rock-and-roll star named Buddy Holly. They went from one town to the next on a bus. The bus's heating system did not work, and it was very cold. One of the band members got frostbite, and Ritchie caught a bad cold. Buddy Holly finally wearied of riding the bus, so he rented a small plane to go to the next town on the tour. He asked Ritchie if he would like to fly, too, and Ritchie gladly agreed.

The pilot took off on February 3, 1959. But, the weather was bad, and there was heavy snow. The plane crashed into a field. Everyone on board died. Ritchie was only 17 years old. But, he had made a breakthrough in the world of music. People around America fell in love with a Mexican song, sung in Spanish, thanks to Ritchie.

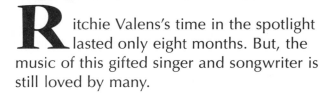

Ritchie Valens
(1941–1959)

Ritchie Valens's time in the spotlight lasted only eight months. But, the music of this gifted singer and songwriter is still loved by many.

Born Ricardo Steven Valenzuela, Ritchie grew up in California. He heard a lot of Mexican music during his childhood, and he loved it. But, he also liked other kinds of music. He listened to the blues. Later, he grew to love rock and roll.

By the time Ritchie was five years old, he wanted to play music of his own. His father helped him. Ritchie got an old guitar. He was left-handed. The guitar was for right-handed people. But, Ritchie wanted to play so badly that he taught himself how to play the guitar anyway. Ritchie also taught himself how to play the drums. He started to write his own **lyrics**. But, Ritchie was quiet and shy. He did not like to show off. Would he be able to play in front of people?

When Ritchie was 16 years old, he joined a band. The band played at dances. Sometimes, the band played at parties, too. When the band's lead singer quit, Ritchie became the singer. This helped him feel less shy in front of people.

The next year, 1958, was a big year for Ritchie. A record producer named Bob Keane came to hear him play. He wanted Ritchie to make a record. By September, Ritchie's songs were heard around the country. One song was called "Donna." It was about a girl Ritchie liked. It was a big hit. But, a different song is the one remembered best today. Ritchie's cousin taught him a Mexican song called

"La Bamba." The song was played at weddings and dances. Musicians wrote their own lyrics for the song, but some of the words were always the same. Ritchie added a new beat to the tune. He made a joyful, fast, fun song. Ritchie sang the song in Spanish.

Ritchie went on a tour. He played in concerts with another rock-and-roll star named Buddy Holly. They went from one town to the next on a bus. The bus was awful. The heating system did not work, and it was very cold. One of the band members got frostbite. Ritchie caught a bad cold. Buddy Holly finally got tired of riding the bus. He rented a small plane. He asked Ritchie if he would like to fly to the next town on the tour with him. Ritchie said yes.

The pilot took off on February 3, 1959. But, the weather was bad. It was snowing hard. The plane crashed into a field. Everyone on board died. Ritchie was only 17 years old. But, he had made a breakthrough in the world of music. People around America fell in love with a Mexican song, sung in Spanish. That was thanks to Ritchie.

Ritchie Valens
(1941–1959)

1. This passage tells about:

   a. a man who wanted to be a blues guitar player.

   b. a 17-year-old Hispanic American who became a rock-and-roll star.

   c. a musician who made an old Mexican song into a rock-and-roll hit.

   d. b and c

2. What does the word **lyrics** mean in the passage?

   a. a type of musical instrument

   b. a unit of Italian money

   c. a kind of cart

   d. the words to a song

3. Number the following events in the order they happened.

   _____ Ritchie grew up in California.

   _____ Ritchie taught himself to play the guitar and drums.

   _____ Ritchie went on a concert tour with Buddy Holly.

   _____ Ritchie became the lead singer in a band.

   _____ Ritchie recorded his first record.

4. Answer the following questions.

   Who was Bob Keane?

   _____

   _____

   How old was Ritchie when he started to play in a band?

   _____

   What girl did Ritchie write about in a song?

   _____

   In what language did Ritchie sing "La Bamba"?

   _____

5. How did Ritchie change the song "La Bamba"?

   a. He wrote English words for it.

   b. He played it in a very slow, soft way.

   c. He added a fast, rock-and-roll beat to the song.

   d. He turned it into a song to which people could dance.

Bonus

Do you like to sing, play music, or speak in front of people? Write a paragraph telling why you do or do not like to do one of these things for an audience.

Pat Mora
(1942– ____)

Pat Mora grew up in El Paso, Texas, near the border between Texas and Mexico. Her parents saw that she had a talent for words. When she finished the eighth grade, they gave Pat a typewriter as a gift, but she did not write for years. She wrote little notes to herself with ideas for books and poems. Then, when she neared the age of 40, Pat started to write, and write, and write.

Pat writes many poems. She says that a poet is a healer, a person who builds bridges between people so that they can relate to the same ideas. Pat feels that she plays this part as a Hispanic woman and an American. She writes in English but uses Spanish words throughout her stories and poems to honor her Mexican heritage. She also sets many of her books in the southwestern United States.

One of her best-known children's books is a tall tale about Doña Flor. Doña Flor is so gigantic that she can pick the stars from the sky like flowers. Children use her tortillas for rafts on the river. She is *una amiga*, a friend, to the whole village. One day, the villagers need her to keep them safe from a fierce animal. Doña Flor is brave, so she goes to find the frightening animal—but instead discovers a secret that is not scary at all.

Pat makes writing her wonderful books look easy, but it was not easy for her to get started. She found that it is very hard for a new writer to get her books published. It took her eight years to get her first book for children printed. It was turned down 25 times!

What does Pat tell writers about writing? She says that it is important for them to make time for writing and to read as many books as they can. She thinks that rewriting work can help polish it, even if this is not as fun as writing a story the first time. Pat also states that a writer should welcome his ideas like guests into his home, because a writer needs to love his writing in order to write well. Pat says that her favorite book is always the one she is going to write next—that is the book she is most excited about.

One of Pat's favorite things to do is visit schools. She believes in "book joy," the great feeling of reading and learning new things. Reading was always important to her, so she wants students to love reading, too. Pat helped bring a Mexican **tradition** to the United States. She learned in 1996 that April 30 is the Day of the Child in Mexico. In the United States, Pat linked this day to children's books and reading. Now, libraries and schools in 15 states celebrate this day, thanks to Pat's hard work. Someday, Pat hopes to bring this day of book joy to everyone in the country.

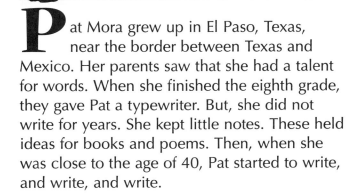

Pat Mora
(1942– _____)

Pat Mora grew up in El Paso, Texas, near the border between Texas and Mexico. Her parents saw that she had a talent for words. When she finished the eighth grade, they gave Pat a typewriter. But, she did not write for years. She kept little notes. These held ideas for books and poems. Then, when she was close to the age of 40, Pat started to write, and write, and write.

Pat writes many poems. She says that a poet is a healer. A poet builds bridges between people so that they can talk about the same ideas. Pat feels that she plays this part as a Hispanic woman and an American. She writes in English. But, she uses Spanish words in her stories and poems to honor her Mexican background. She also sets many of her books in the southwestern United States.

One of her best-known children's books is a tall tale about Doña Flor. Doña Flor is so big that she can pick the stars from the sky like flowers. The children use her tortillas for rafts on the river. She is *una amiga*, a friend, to the whole village. One day, they need her to keep them safe from a wild animal. Doña Flor is brave. She goes to find the scary animal. But instead, she finds a funny secret that is not scary at all.

Pat makes writing her wonderful books look easy. But, it was not easy to get started. She found that it is very hard for a new writer to get books published. It took her eight years to get her first book for children printed. It was turned down 25 times!

What does Pat tell writers about writing? She says that it is important for them to make time for writing. It is also important for them to read as many books as they can. She thinks that rewriting work can make it better, even if it is not as fun as writing a story the first time. Pat also believes that a writer should welcome his ideas like guests into his home. A writer needs to love his writing to write well. Pat says that her favorite book is always the one she is going to write next. It is the book she is most excited about.

One of Pat's favorite things to do is visit schools. She believes in "book joy," the great feeling of reading and learning new things. Reading was always important to her. She wants students to love reading, too. Pat helped bring a Mexican **tradition** to the United States. April 30 is the Day of the Child in Mexico. Pat learned about this in 1996. She linked this day to children's books and reading. Libraries and schools in 15 states now celebrate this day, thanks to Pat's hard work. Someday, Pat hopes to bring this day of book joy to everyone in the country.

Hispanic American Achievers

69

© Carson-Dellosa • CD-104256

Pat Mora
(1942– _____)

1. The first paragraph is mainly about:

   a. how Pat started to write.

   b. why Pat likes to visit schools.

   c. one of Pat's books.

   d. why Pat likes to write poetry.

2. What does the word **tradition** mean in the passage?

   a. a custom that is passed down by a family or group of people

   b. to walk heavily

   c. to trap something or someone

   d. to change a piece of writing from one language to another

3. Number the following events in the order they happened.

   _____ Pat started writing poems.

   _____ Pat's first book was turned down 25 times.

   _____ Pat grew up in the southwestern United States.

   _____ Pat's first children's book came out.

   _____ Pat brought the Day of the Child to the United States.

4. Answer the following questions.

   Why does Pat feel that poets are healers?

   _____

   _____

   How old was Pat when she started to write?

   _____

   Who is Doña Flor?

   _____

   _____

   When was Pat given a typewriter?

   _____

5. Which one of these things is Pat's way of honoring her Mexican background?

   a. She writes poetry and books for children.

   b. She has gone back to Mexico to live.

   c. She uses Spanish words in her stories.

   d. none of the above

Bonus

Choose a country about which you would like to learn. Use books or Web sites to learn some words from that country's language. Write a paragraph about the words that you discover.

Isabel Allende
(1942– _____)

Isabel Allende was born in Chile, but she spent part of her childhood in other parts of the world. Her stepfather was a diplomat, a person who works with other governments. For a time, Isabel went to school in the Middle East.

When she grew up, Isabel lived in Belgium and worked for the United Nations. Then, she went home to Chile. She had a job as a writer for a children's magazine. She also helped write TV shows. But in 1973, something terrible occurred. The government of Chile was overthrown, and the president was killed. The president was Isabel's uncle.

Her family was in danger and knew that they had to leave the country. This broke Isabel's heart. She had to leave behind some people in her family, including her grandfather. He was 93 years old when she left.

Isabel started to write a letter to her grandfather. She wanted him to know that she would never forget him. She would never forget the stories he told her about their family. Her letter grew longer and longer. Finally, Isabel realized that she was writing a **novel**. She named it *The House of the Spirits*. It came out when she was 40 years old.

Isabel has written many books that are now read around the world. Most of the books are for adults, but in 2002, Isabel completed her first children's novel. The book is about a young boy named Alexander Cold. He takes a trip down the Amazon River, meets a strange tribe called the People of the Mists, and learns their secrets. The book is titled *The City of Beasts*. Isabel has also written two other novels about Alexander's adventures.

Today, Isabel lives in California. She became an American citizen in 2003. She said that she did not feel like an American until the sad day of September 11, 2001. For her, it felt like a tie to the sad times she lived through in Chile. But, she says that in many ways, the United States is foreign to her. She says that people here always feel like they can start over. They can move and start a new life. Even though Isabel has moved many times, she still feels linked to Chile. She still writes about her homeland. She says that she cannot leave her past behind, and she does not want to.

Isabel continues to write many different types of books and articles for adults and children. Her magical, descriptive language helps bring her stories to life for readers. Through her writing, she hopes to bridge the divisions between different cultures.

Isabel Allende
(1942– _____)

Isabel Allende was born in Chile. But, she spent part of her childhood in other parts of the world. Her stepfather worked with other governments. For a time, Isabel went to school in the Middle East.

When she grew up, Isabel lived in Belgium. She worked for the United Nations. Then, she went home to Chile. She had a job as a writer for a children's magazine. She also helped write TV shows. But in 1973, something bad happened. The government of Chile was taken over. The president was killed. He was Isabel's uncle.

She and her family were in danger. They had to leave the country. This broke Isabel's heart. She had to leave behind some people in her family. One of them was her grandfather. He was 93 years old when she left.

Isabel started to write a letter to her grandfather. She wanted him to know that she would never forget him. She would never forget the stories he told her. Her letter grew longer and longer. Isabel saw one day that she was writing a **novel**. She named it *The House of the Spirits*. It came out when she was 40 years old.

Isabel has written many books. They are now read around the world. Most of the books are for grown-ups. But in 2002, Isabel wrote her first children's book. The book is about a young boy named Alexander Cold. He takes a trip down the Amazon River. He meets a strange tribe called the People of the Mists. He learns their secrets. The book is called *The City of Beasts*. Isabel has also written two other books about Alexander's adventures.

Today, Isabel lives in California. She became an American in 2003. She said that she did not really feel like she could be an American until the sad day of September 11, 2001. For her, it felt like a tie to the sad times she lived through in Chile. But, she says that in many ways, the United States is strange to her. She says that people here always feel like they can start over. They can move and start a new life. Isabel has moved many times. But, she still feels tied to Chile. She still writes about her homeland. She says that she cannot leave her past behind. And, she does not want to.

Isabel still writes many different types of books and articles for adults and children. Her magical, descriptive words help bring her stories to life for readers. Through her writing, she hopes to bridge the gaps between different cultures.

Isabel Allende
(1942– _____)

1. This passage is mostly about:

   a. a girl who ran away from home.

   b. a writer who made her home in a new country.

   c. an American who went to live in Chile.

   d. the daughter of the president of Chile.

2. What does the word **novel** mean in the passage?

   a. something new

   b. something unusual or strange

   c. a short piece of writing that rhymes

   d. a long story with chapters

3. Number the following events in the order they happened.

   _____ Isabel lived in Belgium and worked for the United Nations.

   _____ Isabel wrote *The House of the Spirits*.

   _____ Isabel's family had to leave Chile.

   _____ Isabel had a job writing for a children's magazine.

   _____ Isabel became an American.

4. Answer the following questions.

   How did Isabel start to write her first book?

   _____

   _____

   What was one part of the world where Isabel lived as a child?

   _____

   Who was the president of Chile?

   _____

   In what year did Isabel write her first book for children?

   _____

5. Why did Isabel feel differently about the United States after September 11, 2001?

   a. She thought that Americans felt the same kind of sadness she had in Chile.

   b. She felt that the sad day of September 11, 2001, drew everyone closer.

   c. She thought that September 11, 2001, was not like any other day in American history.

   d. none of the above

Bonus

Who is one of your favorite family members? Write a letter to that person telling about your feelings for him or her.

Antonia Novello
(1944– ____)

If Antonia Novello had been healthy as a child, she might not have become a doctor. But, Antonia was born with a serious condition of the colon. She spent at least two weeks every year in the hospital, and the doctors became her friends. Finally, when she was 18, she learned that she could have an operation to fix her problem. After her surgery, however, she had complications that lasted for two years.

During this time, Antonia went to school. Her mother did not give her another choice. Her mother was a principal and made sure that Antonia always had the best teachers and the best opportunities. Even when Antonia was not feeling well, she had to do her best.

When Antonia was 20 years old, she went from her home in Puerto Rico to the Mayo Clinic, a famous hospital in the United States. She had another operation there. This time, Antonia was well when she left the hospital. She said that she did not want anyone else to suffer as she had for so many years. After her last operation, she earned her bachelor's degree. She started medical school in 1970.

When she was a doctor, Antonia got a job working for the government. She tried being a children's doctor, but she was too emotional about her patients. She once said that she cried as much as the parents did! So instead, she got a job doing **research**. She researched AIDS, studying the disease in children. She also worked with members of Congress, helping them obtain information about illnesses when they drafted laws about medicine and health care.

In 1990, Antonia was called to the office of the secretary of health. He asked Antonia if she knew why she was in his office. She thought that he had called her in to look at budgets and the way she handled money for her work. But, he told Antonia that President George H. W. Bush wanted her to be the next surgeon general.

The surgeon general is the most important doctor in the country. Antonia was the first Hispanic American to ever hold this job. She was also the first woman to hold this job. During her time in office, Antonia worked on several important medical issues, most of them involving children. She worked to get shots for all children starting school. She campaigned to help students understand why they should not smoke. Today, she works for the state of New York. She still helps people and teaches about health and better medicine.

Antonia Novello
(1944– _____)

If Antonia Novello had been healthy as a child, she might not have become a doctor. But, Antonia was born with a colon problem. She spent at least two weeks every year in the hospital. The doctors became her friends. Then, she learned that she could have an operation to fix her problem. She was 18. After her operation, she had more problems. These lasted for two more years.

During this time, Antonia went to school. Her mother did not give her another choice. Her mother was a principal. She made sure that Antonia had the best teachers. Even when she was not feeling well, she had to do her best.

When Antonia was 20 years old, she went from her home in Puerto Rico to the Mayo Clinic. This is a well-known hospital in the United States. Antonia had another surgery. This time, she was well when she left the hospital. She said that she did not want anyone else to suffer as she had for so many years. She got her bachelor's degree after her last surgery. She started medical school in 1970.

Then, Antonia got a job working for the government. She tried being a children's doctor. But, she was too sad for her patients. She once said that she cried as much as the parents did! So, she got a job doing **research**. One of the things she researched was AIDS. She studied the disease in children. She also worked with members of Congress. She helped them get information about illnesses when they wrote laws about medicine.

In 1990, Antonia was called to the office of the secretary of health. He asked Antonia if she knew why she was in his office. She thought that he had called her in to look at budgets and the way she handled money for her work. But, he told Antonia that President George H. W. Bush wanted her to be the next surgeon general.

The surgeon general is the top doctor in the country. Antonia was the first Hispanic American to hold this important job. She was also the first woman to hold this job. During her time in office, Antonia worked on several important issues. Many of them involved children. She worked to get shots for all children starting school. She worked to help students understand why they should not smoke. Today, she works for the state of New York. She still helps people and teaches about health and better medicine.

Antonia Novello
(1944– ____)

1. Which of the following words best describes Antonia Novello?

   a. weak

   b. caring

   c. lazy

   d. shy

2. What does the word **research** mean in the passage?

   a. the act of looking again for a lost item

   b. the collection and study of information

   c. the creation of laws to help people

   d. the discovery of a new place

3. Number the following events in the order they happened.

   _____ Antonia was born.

   _____ Antonia went to the United States for a second operation.

   _____ Antonia became a doctor.

   _____ Antonia started working for the state of New York.

   _____ Antonia became the United States surgeon general.

4. Answer the following questions.

   What was Antonia's home country?

   _____

   How did Antonia's mother help with her education?

   _____

   _____

   Which president wanted Antonia to become the surgeon general?

   _____

   What was one thing that Antonia worked on as surgeon general?

   _____

   _____

5. What was a good thing that came from Antonia's childhood illness?

   a. She learned a lot about her disease.

   b. She realized that if she became a doctor, she could help other people with illnesses.

   c. She found out that she was not as ill as she thought she had been.

   d. She learned how to do research about different illnesses.

Bonus

What do you think would be the best thing about being a doctor? What would be the hardest thing? Write about your ideas and feelings.

Judy Baca
(1946– _____)

When Judy Baca was young, her mother drew small portraits of her. Judy watched her Mexican grandmother create lace pictures of flowers. When she went to school for the first time, Judy also got to paint for the first time. She made big paintings that were as large as herself. It was her favorite thing to do.

But, Judy never dreamed that she could grow up to be an artist; she did not know that that could even happen. Judy had never seen a museum, she had no training in art, and it was not until she went to college and took an art history class that she first saw paintings, sculptures, and **murals**. She thought then that she could learn about art and become a teacher.

Then, Judy had a chance to create art and teach at the same time. In 1974, she was asked to do paintings on a long concrete wall that was a part of a flood control channel in Los Angeles, California. Judy started to paint. She wanted to assemble a history of California, showing all of the people who are often left out of history books. In 1976, a group of troubled teens came to work with Judy on the paintings. So did other artists and several historians. Every summer after that, the painting grew longer and longer.

The huge painting, which people called *The Great Wall of Los Angeles*, was completed in 1984. It is the longest **mural** in the world. More than 700 people helped Judy paint the mural. It shows the Hispanic Americans who worked on California's railroads. It shows the struggle for civil rights by people like Rosa Parks. It shows Japanese Americans who were sent to camps during World War II. It is a painting of how people of all races built the state together.

Today, Judy plans other mural projects in Los Angeles. She started this work in 1988. She finds walls where people can paint murals. Then, she finds kids in the neighborhood to work on the paintings with artists.

Most murals stay in one place, but Judy created a mural that is traveling around the world. It is called *The World Wall*, and it is a call for world peace and for countries to help each other. This mural is made of panels that can be taken apart. The entire mural is shipped to one country after another. In each new country, artists add panels of their own.

Judy Baca
(1946– _____)

When Judy Baca was young, her mother drew pictures of her. Judy watched her Mexican grandmother make lace pictures of flowers. When she went to school for the first time, she also got to paint for the first time. She made big paintings, as large as herself. It was her favorite thing to do.

But, Judy never thought that she could grow up to be an artist. She did not know that that could happen. Judy had never seen a museum. She had no training in art. She saw works of art for the first time when she went to college. She took an art history class. She thought that she could learn about art. Then, she could be a teacher.

Then, Judy had a chance to paint and teach at the same time. It was 1974. Judy was asked to do a painting on a long wall. The wall was in Los Angeles, California. It was a part of a channel for flood water. Judy started to paint. She wanted to tell the story of California. She wanted to show people who are not always in history books.

In 1976, a big group of teenagers came to work with Judy. So did other artists and history teachers. They all worked on the painting together. Every summer, the painting got longer.

The huge painting was done in 1984. People called it *The Great Wall of Los Angeles*. It is the longest **mural** in the world. More than 700 people worked with Judy on the painting. It shows Hispanic Americans who worked on the railroad. It shows the fight for civil rights. It shows Japanese Americans who were sent to camps during World War II. It tells how people of all races built the state together.

Today, Judy plans other mural paintings in Los Angeles. She started this work in 1988. She finds walls where people can paint murals. Then, she finds kids in the neighborhood to work with artists. They make the paintings together.

Most murals stay in one place. But, Judy made one mural that is going around the world. It is called *The World Wall*. It is about world peace. This mural is made of panels. They can be taken apart. The mural is sent to one country after another. In each new country, artists add panels of their own.

Judy Baca
(1946– _____)

1. What is the main idea of the last paragraph?

   a. Judy painted a mural about California that is being sent around the world.

   b. Judy is sending a mural that she started around the world so that other artists can add to it.

   c. Judy found a mural, took it apart, and started to send pieces of it around the world.

   d. Judy started a mural about world peace at the United Nations headquarters.

2. What does the word **mural** mean in the passage?

   a. a large, shaped piece of art which is put in a plaza

   b. a large piece of paper that is painted in many colors

   c. a large painting that can take up a whole wall

   d. a large cloth on which artists paint

3. Number the following events in the order they happened.

   _____ Judy painted for the first time.

   _____ Judy set up *The World Wall*, a traveling mural.

   _____ Judy studied to become a teacher.

   _____ Judy started painting *The Great Wall of Los Angeles*.

   _____ Judy started helping neighborhoods in Los Angeles, California, make their own murals.

4. Answer the following questions.

   Where did Judy learn about the history of art?

   _____

   How many people helped Judy paint *The Great Wall of Los Angeles*?

   _____

   What story does *The Great Wall of Los Angeles* tell?

   _____

   _____

   Who drew pictures of Judy when she was a child?

   _____

5. What is the theme of *The World Wall*?

   a. Its theme is to show how every country is on its own.

   b. Its theme is peace between countries of the world.

   c. Its theme is the wars that have been fought around the world.

   d. all of the above

Bonus

Imagine that your neighborhood is going to paint a mural. What would you want the painting to show? What story would it tell?

Bill Richardson
(1947– _____)

Bill Richardson was born in California, but he grew up in Mexico City, Mexico. His father was from an old Boston, Massachusetts, family and worked as a banker. His mother was from Mexico. So was Bill's grandmother.

Growing up, Bill led the life of a wealthy man's son, but he also knew about the problems of poor people in Mexico City. One day, a boy carrying two buckets came to Bill's house. He asked for water. Bill asked him to stay and play. They played in the big, walled garden of Bill's house. Then, his new friend, Ernesto, took Bill outside the walls to the "lost city." This was what people called the slums of Mexico City. The slums were where Ernesto lived.

When Bill was 13, he was sent to Boston, where he attended the same expensive schools where his father and grandfather had studied. Bill loved baseball and was able to play on the college team.

Bill always knew that he would spend his life serving other people. In 1982, he won a seat in the U.S. Congress for the state of New Mexico. Bill spent 14 years in Congress. During that time, he helped Hispanic Americans and American Indians. Bill also went to Iraq twice to negotiate with Saddam Hussein, asking him to release Americans who were held in jail there.

Bill's meetings with Saddam were tense and frightening. During his first meeting, Bill sat down and crossed his legs. This showed the bottom of one of his shoes. Saddam jumped from his seat and stormed out of the room. Bill discovered that showing someone the sole of your shoe is an insult in Iraq. At other times, Bill went to Cuba and North Korea to ask for the release of **hostages** in those countries.

In 1997, Bill was appointed as ambassador to the United Nations. The next year, President Bill Clinton asked Bill to be his secretary of energy. In this position, Bill worked to make nuclear plants safer. He tried to convince people to look for new ways to create power from better sources.

The next step in Bill's career was to run for governor. He was elected governor of New Mexico in 2002. He went around the state to ask for votes. One day while campaigning, he shook more than 13,000 hands!

Bill is best known for two things. First, he is very friendly and would rather hug people than shake their hands. Second, he is filled with energy. He always wants to get new things done and never thinks negatively. Some people think that this man with the big smile will someday become the first Hispanic American president of the United States.

Bill Richardson
(1947– _____)

Bill Richardson was born in California. But, he grew up in Mexico City, Mexico. His father was from an old Boston, Massachusetts, family. He worked as a banker. His mother was from Mexico. So was Bill's grandmother.

Growing up, Bill led the life of a rich man's son. But, he also knew about the problems of the poor people around him. One day, a boy carrying two buckets came to Bill's house. He asked for water. Bill asked him to stay and play. They played in the big, walled garden of Bill's house. But, Ernesto also took Bill outside the walls to the "lost city." This was what people called the slums of Mexico City. This was where Ernesto lived.

Then, Bill turned 13. He went to Boston. There, he went to the same costly schools where his father and grandfather had gone. Bill loved baseball. He played on the college team.

Bill always knew that he would spend his life serving other people. In 1982, he won a seat in the U.S. Congress. He worked for the state of New Mexico. Bill spent 14 years in Congress. He helped Hispanic Americans and American Indians. He was also sent to Iraq twice. There, he asked Saddam Hussein to free Americans who were held in jail.

Bill's meetings with Saddam were scary. Bill sat down and crossed his legs during the first meeting. This showed the bottom of one of his shoes. Saddam jumped from his seat. He stormed out of the room. Bill found out that showing the sole of his shoe was an insult in Iraq. Bill also went to Cuba and North Korea to ask for the release of **hostages** there.

In 1997, Bill was named the ambassador to the United Nations. The next year, President Bill Clinton asked Bill to be his secretary of energy. Bill worked to make nuclear plants safer. He tried to convince people to look for new ways to make power from better sources.

The next step for Bill was to run for governor. He was elected governor of New Mexico in 2002. He went around the state to ask for votes. One day, he shook more than 13,000 hands!

Bill is best known for two things. First, he is very friendly. He would rather hug people than shake their hands. Second, he is filled with energy. He always wants to get new things done. Some people think that this man with the big smile will someday be the first Hispanic American president of the United States.

Bill Richardson
(1947– _____)

1. What is the main idea of the second paragraph?

   a. Bill is the son of a Boston, Massachusetts, banker.

   b. Bill ran for the U.S. Congress for the state of New Mexico.

   c. Bill grew up in a rich home, but he knew about the problems of the poor.

   d. Bill went to several countries to try to free hostages.

2. What does the word **hostages** mean in the passage?

   a. people who are very angry

   b. people who are sent to represent another country

   c. people who are held as prisoners in another country

   d. people who try to get other people out of jail

3. Number the following events in the order they happened.

   _____ Bill played baseball on his college team.

   _____ Bill ran for governor of New Mexico.

   _____ Bill ran for the U.S. Congress for New Mexico.

   _____ Bill was born to an American father and a Mexican mother.

   _____ Bill grew up in Mexico City, Mexico.

4. Answer the following questions.

   Where did Bill grow up?

   _____

   What happened to Bill when he was 13 years old?

   _____

   _____

   When did Bill become governor of New Mexico?

   _____

   What job did President Bill Clinton ask Bill to do?

   _____

5. Why do you think it was important for Bill to know Ernesto?

   a. Ernesto helped Bill see how poor people lived.

   b. Ernesto taught Bill how to play baseball.

   c. Ernesto showed Bill the wealthy part of Mexico City.

   d. Ernesto was Bill's only friend.

Bonus

Imagine that you are elected governor. You are in charge of your entire state! What is the first thing you would do? Why?

France Anne Córdova
(1947– _____)

France Córdova learned about juggling many things at once when she was young. She was the oldest child in her family and had 11 brothers and sisters! France had to take care of them, but she also had to do her schoolwork. So, she did both. She helped her parents manage the household; she became a top student; and when she had extra time, she read Nancy Drew mysteries. She loved reading the clues and trying to find the **solutions**.

France tried many different studies and careers as she grew up. She studied English in college. Would she teach literature? Then, she went on a dig in Mexico. Would she become an archaeologist? France loved learning about her Mexican heritage, and she wrote a cookbook of traditional Mexican recipes. She also wrote a novel. Would she become a full-time writer? In the end, stars and planets seized her attention. When France saw the *Apollo 11* astronauts taking their first steps on the moon, she fell in love with the idea of studying space.

France went back to school to study the science of space. She worked in a laboratory, then taught astrophysics. In 1993, France was selected to be the chief scientist at the National Aeronautics and Space Administration (NASA). She was the first woman ever to have this job. It allowed her to focus on space and the stars full-time.

One thing that France has studied in her career is the pulsar. Pulsars are small pieces that remain and glow in space after a star explodes. France is also interested in where we might find other life in the universe. She feels that we should first look closely at Mars. It is near the sun, and there are signs that Mars once had water. France also thinks that Titan, a moon of Saturn, might have signs of life since it may

have a strange form of frozen ocean. One of the satellites of Jupiter, named Europa, may also have ice or water on its surface.

In 2002, France became chancellor of the University of California at Riverside. Then in 2007, she became president of Purdue University. She feels strongly about education and about science. She wants more girls to study science, and she wants to aid minority students in getting a better education. She knows that it can be difficult. As she went through school, many people told her that her goals were impossible—but every step of the way, France proved them wrong.

France has always been happy with her choice of a scientific career. She says that there are many puzzles and mysteries in space. Just like Nancy Drew, she follows the clues and helps uncover some of the answers.

France Anne Córdova
(1947– _____)

France Córdova learned about taking care of many things at once when she was young. She was the oldest child in her family. She had 11 brothers and sisters! France had to help take care of them. But, she also had to do her schoolwork. So, she did both. She helped her parents run their home. She also became a top student. And, when she had extra time, she read Nancy Drew mysteries. She loved reading the clues and finding the **solutions**.

France tried many different studies and jobs as she grew up. She studied English in college. Would she teach about stories and poems? Then, she went on a dig in Mexico. Would she become an archaeologist? France loved learning about her Mexican background, and she wrote a book of recipes from Mexico. She also wrote a novel. Would she become a full-time writer? In the end, the stars and planets got her attention. When France saw the *Apollo 11* astronauts taking their first steps on the moon, she fell in love with the idea of studying space.

France went back to school to study space science. She worked in a lab. Then, she taught astrophysics. In 1993, France was hired to be the chief scientist at the National Aeronautics and Space Administration (NASA). She was the first woman ever to have this job. It let her study space and the stars full-time.

One thing that France has studied in her career is the pulsar. Pulsars are small pieces that glow in space after a star explodes. Another thing that interests France is where we might find other life in the universe. She feels that we should first look closely at Mars. It is close to the sun. There are signs that show Mars once had water. France also thinks that Titan, a moon of Saturn, might have signs of life. It may have a strange kind of frozen ocean. One of the satellites of Jupiter, called Europa, may also have ice or water.

In 2002, France became chancellor of the University of California at Riverside. Then in 2007, she became president of Purdue University. She feels strongly about learning and about science. She wants more girls to study science. She wants to help minorities get better schooling. She knows that it can be hard. When she went to school, many people told her that her goals were impossible. But, every step of the way, France proved them wrong.

France has always been happy with her choice to work in the field of science. She says that there are many puzzles and mysteries in space. Just like Nancy Drew, she follows the clues. She helps find some of the answers.

France Anne Córdova
(1947– _____)

1. What is the main idea of the second paragraph?

   a. France tried many different studies and jobs before choosing science.

   b. France never made up her mind about what to do with her life.

   c. France was able to help her parents and stay a top student.

   d. France loved to read and write.

2. What does the word **solution** mean in the passage?

   a. a mixture made in a lab

   b. something you use to wash your hands

   c. an answer or explanation

   d. a paid debt

3. Number the following events in the order they happened.

   _____ France became the chief scientist at NASA.

   _____ France became chancellor of the University of California at Riverside.

   _____ France went to Mexico on a dig.

   _____ France helped take care of all of her brothers and sisters.

   _____ France chose to study space science.

4. Answer the following questions.

   What was *Apollo 11*?

   _____

   _____

   How many brothers and sisters did France have?

   _____

   What are pulsars?

   _____

   _____

   What is one place where France thinks we may find signs of life in the universe?

   _____

5. Why does the author compare France to Nancy Drew at the end of the passage?

   a. France used to read Nancy Drew mysteries as a girl.

   b. France became a detective and has solved many crimes.

   c. France solves mysteries about space the way that Nancy Drew solves mysteries in stories.

   d. a and c

Bonus

Is there a mystery about space that you would like to solve? Write about it. How do you think it might be solved?

Horacio Gutiérrez
(1948– _____)

Horacio Gutiérrez had a mother who played the piano. His mother started to teach him music when he was a toddler and had just started to walk. The little boy loved the piano, and he was soon studying with a famous Spanish composer named Joaquin Nin. Horacio was only 11 years old when he played with an orchestra for the first time in the city of Havana, Cuba.

Horacio's happy family lived in Cuba. But, things in Cuba were changing. There was a revolution, and a new leader named Fidel Castro took power. At first, Horacio's parents thought that Castro would be a good leader. But after two years, life had become frightening and difficult. Many people were arrested. There were shootings and attacks. Horacio's family felt that escape was necessary. First, they went to Columbia. Then, they traveled to the United States and went to live in Los Angeles, California. Horacio became a U.S. citizen in 1967, when he was 18 years old.

Horacio kept playing the piano and studied with another famous teacher. This teacher, named Sergey Tarnowsky, was from Russia. Then, Horacio was given a place at Juilliard, the best-known music school in the nation. Horacio was pleased to have such good teachers, but he said that a tape recorder is an excellent teacher, too. He thinks that everyone who learns to play the piano needs to listen to herself play. That way, she can hear her mistakes and fix what does not work.

Horacio thinks a lot about the music that he plays, trying to **capture** the mood behind each piece of music. He reflects on the parts of a piece of music and how they fit together. Today, Horacio plays with groups around the world and creates recordings of his performances. He also won a very important award, the Avery Fisher Award, in 1982. This prize has been won by only a few musicians, even though it was created in 1974.

One thing that Horacio likes is new music. He likes to play the music of composers who are working today. Often, the works of these composers do not get much attention. But, Horacio plays their pieces in different concerts so that the public can hear them. A composer named George Perle has written music just for Horacio to perform.

Horacio says that pianists tend to be loners. A pianist has to spend long hours alone and does not practice often with a big group, like an orchestra. A pianist also has to spend a lot of time thinking about the music he works on. It helps Horacio to have other pianists as friends. Horacio is even married to another pianist, and he says it helps that they understand and enjoy each other's work.

Horacio Gutiérrez
(1948– ____)

Horacio Gutiérrez had a mother who played the piano. His mother started to teach him music when he had just started to walk. The little boy loved the piano. Soon, he was studying with a famous Spanish composer named Joaquin Nin. Horacio was only 11 years old when he played with an orchestra for the first time. This was in the city of Havana, Cuba.

Horacio's happy family lived in Cuba. But, things in Cuba were changing. There was a revolution. A new leader named Fidel Castro took over. At first, Horacio's mother and father thought that Castro would be a good leader. But, after two years, life had become scary. Many people were arrested. There were shootings and attacks. The family had to escape. First, they went to Columbia. Then, they went to the United States. The family went to live in Los Angeles, California. Horacio became a U.S. citizen in 1967, when he was 18 years old.

Horacio kept playing the piano. He studied with another well-known teacher named Sergey Tarnowsky. He was from Russia. Then, Horacio was given a place at Juilliard. This is the best-known music school in the country. Horacio was happy to have such good teachers. But, he said that a tape recorder is a good teacher, too. He thinks that everyone who learns to play the piano needs to listen to herself play. That way, she can hear her mistakes. She can fix what does not work.

Horacio thinks a lot about the music that he plays. He tries to **capture** the mood behind each piece of music. He thinks about how the parts of a piece of music fit together. Today, he plays with groups around the world. He makes recordings of his playing. He also won a very important award in 1982. It is called the Avery Fisher Award. It was created in 1974. But, it has been won by only a few musicians.

One thing that Horacio likes is new music. He likes to play the music of composers who are working today. Many times, these composers do not get much attention. But, Horacio plays their pieces in different concerts. A composer named George Perle has written music just for Horacio to play.

Horacio says that pianists are loners. A pianist has to spend long hours alone. He has to think a lot about his music. He does not practice often with a big group, like an orchestra. It helps Horacio to have other pianists as friends. He is even married to another pianist. Horacio says it helps that they understand and enjoy each other's work.

Horacio Gutiérrez
(1948– _____)

1. Choose a good title for this passage.

    a. The Revolution in Cuba

    b. A Master of the Piano

    c. The Best Teachers of Music

    d. Music around the World

2. What does the word **capture** mean in the passage?

    a. to take another person prisoner

    b. to represent something using skill or talent

    c. to keep promises

    d. to win a contest or election

3. Number the following events in the order they happened.

    _____ Horacio became a U.S. citizen.

    _____ Horacio won the Avery Fisher Award.

    _____ Horacio played the piano for the first time.

    _____ Horacio played onstage in Havana, Cuba, for the first time.

    _____ Horacio studied with a Spanish composer named Joaquin Nin.

4. Answer the following questions.

    Why did Horacio and his family leave Cuba?

    _____

    _____

    What is Juilliard?

    _____

    _____

    Who is George Perle?

    _____

    _____

    Who was Horacio's first piano teacher?

    _____

5. Why does the author say that pianists are "loners"?

    a. Pianists practice alone, often for hours.

    b. Pianists do not get to practice with other musicians very often.

    c. Pianists have to think a lot about the music they are working on.

    d. all of the above

Bonus

What special thing did a family member teach you when you were young? Write a paragraph about it.

88

Sonia Manzano
(1950– _____)

Sesame Street would not feel like the same show without Luis and Maria. A long time ago, these two characters fell in love and had a big wedding on the show. For 20 years, they have fixed toasters and all kinds of other things at the Fix-It Shop. They have a daughter named Gabi. They teach Spanish words, and they talk about Hispanic customs.

But, in real life, Maria is played by Sonia Manzano. Sonia has had an amazing career as an actor and a writer. She works for many charities and causes and has won many awards.

Sonia's parents emigrated from Puerto Rico. Sonia grew up in the South Bronx, near New York City. During school, she studied acting. When she was in college, she won a part in a musical that later became a Broadway hit. The next year, she started acting on *Sesame Street*.

Sonia loved TV shows as a child, but she never saw any role models on the shows—not any who looked like her. There were no parts for Hispanic Americans. But, this was a TV show that wanted to change that. *Sesame Street* wanted to educate children about all of the different people in the world. Sonia wanted to be a part of that; it gave her the opportunity to teach these important lessons to children.

Sonia worked on the TV show for 10 years. Then, she told the people she worked for that she wanted to write as well as act for the show. Sonia started to create portions of the show, including the songs. So far, she has won 15 Emmy® awards as a member of the writing team.

After writing for a children's TV show, it was not a surprise when Sonia wrote her first children's book. It is called *No Dogs Allowed*. The book came out in 2004, and it was made into a play in 2006. This humorous story is about a big family and their friends who go on a trip to the beach. They take everything with them—a huge dinner, a piano, games, and the family dog. After the success of her first book, Sonia wrote another children's story in 2007, **titled** *A Box Full of Kittens*.

Now, Sonia's life is hectic. She lives in New York City. She is writing more books and giving speeches. She has worked for charities that help children, including the March of Dimes. She acts in plays on Broadway. But, she still works as Maria on *Sesame Street*, where she fixes toasters, sings songs, and teaches Spanish to the many children who watch the show every day.

Sonia Manzano
(1950– _____)

Sesame Street would not be the same without Luis and Maria. A long time ago, these two characters fell in love. Their wedding was on the show. For 20 years, they have fixed toasters and other things at the Fix-It Shop. They have a daughter named Gabi. They teach Spanish words. They talk about Hispanic customs.

But, in real life, Maria is played by Sonia Manzano. Sonia has had an amazing career. She is an actor and a writer. She works for many causes. She has won many awards.

Sonia's parents came from Puerto Rico. Sonia grew up in the South Bronx, near New York City. During school, she studied acting. When she was in college, she got a part in a play that later became a hit on Broadway. The next year, she started acting on Sesame Street.

Sonia loved TV shows as a child. But, she never saw anyone on the shows who looked like her. There were no parts for Hispanic Americans. But, this was a TV show that wanted to change that. Sesame Street wanted to teach children about all of the different people in the world. Sonia wanted to be a part of that. It gave her the chance to teach important lessons to children.

Sonia acted on the TV show for 10 years. Then, she told the people she worked for that she wanted to write for the show, too. Sonia started to write parts of the show. She even helped write songs. So far, she has won 15 Emmy® awards as a member of the writing team.

Next, Sonia wrote her first children's book. It is called No Dogs Allowed. The book came out in 2004. In 2006, it was made into a play. It is a funny story. A big family and their friends go on a trip to the beach. They take everything with them—a huge dinner, a piano, games, and the family dog. Sonia wrote another children's book in 2007. It is **titled** A Box Full of Kittens.

Now, Sonia's life is very busy. She lives in New York City. She is working on more books. She gives speeches. She has worked for groups that help children, including the March of Dimes. She acts in plays on Broadway. But, she still works on Sesame Street as Maria. She fixes toasters, sings songs, and teaches Spanish to the many children who watch the show every day.

Sonia Manzano
(1950– ____)

1. Which of the following words best describes Sonia Manzano?

   a. creative

   b. sad

   c. angry

   d. forceful

2. What does the word **titled** mean in the passage?

   a. being royal

   b. having told someone about bad behavior

   c. called or named

   d. being made of tile

3. Number the following events in the order they happened.

   _____   Sonia studied acting in school.

   _____   Sonia started working as a writer for *Sesame Street*.

   _____   Sonia acted in her first major play.

   _____   Sonia wrote her first children's book.

   _____   Sonia got an acting part on *Sesame Street*.

4. Answer the following questions.

   What is *No Dogs Allowed* about?

   _____

   _____

   Who is Maria?

   _____

   _____

   What does Sonia do for the TV show *Sesame Street*?

   _____

   _____

   What is one thing that Sonia does today?

   _____

   _____

5. Besides acting and writing, what else does Sonia do?

   a. She teaches at a college.

   b. She designs clothing.

   c. She works for groups that help children.

   d. all of the above

Bonus

Think about a trip you took with your family or friends. Write a funny story about it.

Ileana Ros-Lehtinen
(1952– _____)

Ileana Ros-Lehtinen was born in Cuba, but when Fidel Castro came into power, her father fought against him. As an enemy of the new leader, Ileana's family had to leave. Ileana was seven years old when she came to Florida. She did not know even one word of English. Her first year of school in the United States was very hard. She struggled to keep up.

When she grew up, Ileana became a teacher. She even helped start her own school in Florida. She kept going to school, too, and eventually earned a PhD in education.

But, Ileana was like her father—politics caught her attention. She ran for the Florida House of Representatives and was elected in 1982, at the age of 30. Then, she became a state senator in 1986. It was during this time that she met her husband. He was in the state **legislature**, too.

The next step for Ileana was a seat in the U.S. Congress. She won that election in 1989 and became the first Hispanic American woman to be elected to the House of Representatives. Ileana has often said that her place in Congress proves that the United States is a great country. After all, she came here without being able to speak English. By working hard and learning all that she could, Ileana is now one of the lawmakers for the entire country.

There are many causes that Ileana wants to advance. One is saving Florida's coastline. Ileana does not want oil companies to drill near Florida and harm the marine life and the reefs. She voted for money to help preserve coral reefs and the animals that live around the coast.

Ileana also voted for plans that help parents save money for their children's college funds, and she has made sure that loans for students are not too expensive. She wants these benefits for the people who voted for her because, as a teacher, she feels that education is crucial.

Ileana also remembers what it was like to sit in a classroom and not understand what was going on. She wants teachers to be able to use Spanish to teach Hispanic American children. She likes programs that let Spanish-speaking children study in Spanish while they also learn English. With lesson plans like that, Ileana says that she would have found school a lot easier.

Another issue that concerns Ileana is the women in Iraq. Ileana took trips to Iraq as a congresswoman. While she was there, she saw that women were worried for their safety. For a long time, the women in Iraq have been treated like second-class citizens. They want a better future as life in their country changes direction. Ileana works to ensure that for them.

Ileana Ros-Lehtinen
(1952– _____)

Ileana Ros-Lehtinen was born in Cuba. But, her father fought against Fidel Castro. When Castro took over the country, Ileana's family had to leave. She was seven years old when she came to Florida. She did not know even one word of English. Her first year of school in the United States was very hard. She struggled to keep up.

When she grew up, Ileana became a teacher. She even helped start her own school in Florida. She kept going to school, too. She got a PhD in education.

But, Ileana was like her father. Politics caught her attention. She ran for the Florida House of Representatives. She was elected in 1982. She was 30 years old. Then, she became a state senator in 1986. It was during this time that she met her husband. He was in the state **legislature**, too.

The next step for Ileana was the U.S. Congress. She won a seat in 1989. She was the first Hispanic American woman to go to Congress. Ileana has often said that her place in Congress shows that the United States is a great country. She came here without being able to speak English. By working hard, she is now able to help make laws for the whole country.

There are many causes that interest Ileana. One is saving Florida's coastline. Ileana does not want oil companies to drill near Florida. It would hurt the sea life and the reefs. She voted for money to help save coral reefs and animals that live around the coast.

Ileana also voted for plans that help parents save money for their children's college funds. She makes sure that loans for students do not cost too much. She wants these things for the people who voted for her. As a teacher, she feels that school is very important.

Ileana also remembers what it was like to sit in a classroom and not know what was going on. She wants teachers to be able to use Spanish to teach Hispanic American children. She likes programs that let Spanish-speaking children study in Spanish while learning English. With schooling like that, Ileana says that she would have found school a lot easier.

Another thing that concerns Ileana is women in Iraq. Ileana took trips to Iraq. While she was there, she saw that women were worried for their safety. Women in Iraq have not been treated well for a long time. They want a better life in their changing country. Ileana works to help them get that.

Ileana Ros-Lehtinen
(1952– _____)

1. The first paragraph is mainly about:

   a. how Ileana chose to be a teacher.

   b. the changes Ileana faced by moving from Cuba to Florida.

   c. why Ileana made the choice to go into politics.

   d. how Ileana works for the women in Iraq.

2. What does the word **legislature** mean in the passage?

   a. a group that takes over a government

   b. a group that does not want others to vote

   c. a group that prints a newspaper

   d. a group that is elected to make laws

3. Number the following events in the order they happened.

   _____ Ileana's family had to run from Fidel Castro.

   _____ Ileana opened her own school.

   _____ Ileana became the first Hispanic American woman in the U.S. Congress.

   _____ Ileana won her first election.

   _____ Ileana was elected to the Florida Senate.

4. Answer the following questions.

   Whom did Ileana meet when she became a Florida state senator?

   _____

   What has Ileana done to help save the Florida coast?

   _____

   _____

   How old was Ileana when she won her first election?

   _____

   Why does Ileana want low-cost loans for students?

   _____

   _____

5. Why does Ileana want teachers to be able to use Spanish to teach?

   a. She knows how it feels to not understand lessons in English.

   b. She thinks that Spanish-speaking children should be able to learn in Spanish.

   c. She wants children to understand lessons while they learn English.

   d. all of the above

Bonus

Read about a senator or representative who serves your state or region. Write a letter to the person asking him or her to support an issue that is important to you.

Gary Soto
(1952– _____)

When Gary Soto was growing up, he thought that he could find a job as a gardener. Or, maybe he could get a job as a farm worker. These are jobs that many Hispanic Americans he knew had. Even when he was young, Gary had to work to help his family. Because of that, he finished high school with very bad grades.

But, it was in high school that Gary started reading a lot of books. He devoured stories, novels, and plays. The more he read, the more he wanted to read. Then, Gary attended a community college. It was there that he started to read poetry and decided that he wanted to be a writer.

Gary began to write his own poems. He won an important award when he was only 23 years old: the American Poets Prize. That same year, 1975, Gary married his wife, Carolyn.

Gary began teaching, and he also kept writing at a fast rate. His first complete book of poems came out in 1977. Ten years later, Gary wrote his first children's story. It is called *The Cat's Meow*. His wife **illustrated** the book. After that, Gary traveled two writing paths: creating poetry for adults and writing stories and novels for kids.

Gary grew up in Fresno, California. Today, he lives in Berkeley, California, where he has taught for many years. But, he goes back to Fresno almost every month. It is the setting for most of his stories and poems. His neighborhood, his friends, and even some members of his own family are in Gary's books and poems. He writes about playing baseball and going to school. He writes about taking fruit from his neighbor's tree and playing in sprinklers. He writes about the factories and junkyards all around him.

What is Gary's favorite book that he has written? It is titled *Jesse*. In the story, Jesse and his brother Abel go to a community college, just as Gary did. The two brothers work in the fields to make money. They worry about being drafted into the army. They also learn about César Chávez's brave stand on behalf of farm workers. Many of Gary's books depict real life for Hispanic Americans in California. They show these families in their struggles, but they also show their strength and love for each other.

Gary says that his favorite occupation is not writing, but reading. He says that reading builds a life inside the mind. He still writes often, though. His wife is the first person to read most of his work. Gary enjoys attending plays, watching tennis and baseball, and working in his garden. But, the most important thing that Gary grows is stories, which he shares with all of his readers.

Gary Soto
(1952– _____)

When Gary Soto was growing up, he thought that he could find a job as a gardener. Or, maybe he could get a job on a farm. These are jobs that many of his friends and neighbors had. Gary had to work to help his family, even when he was young. His grades in high school were very bad because he had to work.

But, in high school, Gary started to read a lot of books. He read stories, novels, and plays. He wanted to read more and more. Gary went to college. Then, he began to read poems. That was when he knew that he wanted to be a writer.

Gary started to write his own poems. He won a big award when he was 23 years old. It is called the American Poets Prize. That same year, 1975, was when Gary married his wife, Carolyn.

Gary got a job as a teacher. He kept writing and writing. His first book of poems came out in 1977. Ten years later, Gary wrote his first children's story. It is called *The Cat's Meow*. His wife **illustrated** the book. Now, he writes poetry for adults and stories for kids.

Gary grew up in Fresno, California. Today, he lives in Berkeley, California. That is where he has taught for many years. But, he goes back to Fresno almost every month. It is the place where most of his poems and stories are set. His neighborhood, his friends, and even some members of his own family are in Gary's books and poems. He writes about playing baseball. He writes about going to school. He writes about taking fruit from his neighbor's tree and playing in sprinklers. He writes about the factories and junkyards all around him.

What is Gary's favorite book that he has written? It is called *Jesse*. In the story, Jesse and his brother Abel go to a local college. They work in the fields to make money. They worry about being drafted into the army. They also learn about César Chávez's brave stand for farm workers. Many of Gary's books tell about life for Hispanic Americans in California. They show how families struggle. They also show how strong they are.

Gary says that his favorite thing to do is read. He says that reading builds a life inside the mind. But, he still writes often. His wife is the first person to read most of his work. He likes going to plays, watching tennis and baseball, and working in his garden. But, the most important thing that Gary grows is stories, which he shares with his readers.

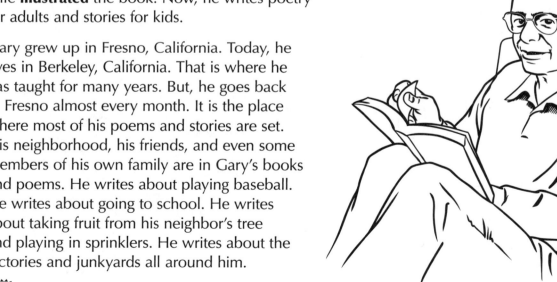

Gary Soto
(1952– _____)

1. Choose a good title for this passage.

   a. The Story of *Jesse*

   b. Farm Workers in California

   c. Growing Up in Fresno, California

   d. How Reading Changed a Life

2. What does the word **illustrated** mean in the passage?

   a. drew pictures for a story

   b. wrote for children

   c. published a book

   d. made up a title for a book

3. Number the following events in the order they happened.

   _____ Gary thought that he could be a gardener or a farm worker.

   _____ Gary wrote *The Cat's Meow.*

   _____ Gary went to college.

   _____ Gary won the American Poets Prize.

   _____ Gary got bad grades in high school.

4. Answer the following questions.

When did Gary know that he wanted to write?

_____

_____

In what year did Gary write his first book for children?

_____

Why is Fresno important in Gary's work?

_____

_____

Why does Gary like reading so much?

_____

_____

5. What is Gary's book *Jesse* about?

   a. It is about two brothers who go to elementary school.

   b. It is about two brothers who go to college and work as farm workers.

   c. It is about two brothers who go into the army together.

   d. none of the above

Bonus

Do you like to read? Why or why not? Write a paragraph explaining the feelings you have when you read a book.

Pedro José "Joe" Greer
(1956– _____)

As the only male left in his Cuban family, Pedro José "Joe" Greer was supposed to take care of his two sisters. But, Joe lost one of his sisters after he had started medical school. She died in a car accident, and Joe felt that he had failed her. He made a promise to himself after her death: he would never let anyone else die alone.

Joe finished medical school. He was working as an **intern**, overseen by a doctor. When a patient he helped treat was dying, Joe went to look for the man's family. The search took him to a homeless shelter called Camillus House. Joe saw how little help the people there had for their medical problems. He set up a free clinic there on his own. That was in 1984.

But, Joe did not stay inside the clinic and wait for patients to come. He roamed the streets. He looked under highway bridges, in trash-filled alleys, and in parks. He found people without homes and told them about the clinic, promising to help them if they went there.

At first, Joe had no help. He paid for supplies on his own. He asked people to donate furniture and medicine. He talked people into helping at the clinic for free. And, the number of sick people who came for help kept growing.

Joe started to request money from the government and charities. This money is called grant money. He became gifted at persuading others to help him keep the clinic open. He was so skilled that he was eventually able to open two more clinics. One was in a neighborhood called Little Havana in Miami, Florida. The other was near a camp for farm workers.

In 1991, Joe joined a special task force. This group helped the government learn more about health care for the poor. That same year, he became the first person to teach about health care for the homeless at a medical school in Miami. Students at the school work at the free clinics so that they can learn more about helping the poor firsthand. Today, Joe's first tiny clinic is an impressive building run by more than 250 workers, 200 of whom give their time for free.

In 1993, Joe was given an important grant, called a "genius grant." Its real name is a MacArthur Fellowship. It is money given to people who use their creativity to solve problems or do important work in the United States. Joe has done both. His aid to the poor has changed the lives of many in Miami.

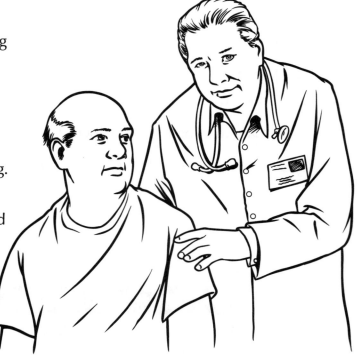

Pedro José "Joe" Greer
(1956– _____)

As the only male left in his Cuban family, Pedro José "Joe" Greer was supposed to take care of his two sisters. But, Joe lost one of his sisters. It was after he had started medical school. His sister died in a car accident. Joe felt that he had failed her. He made a promise after her death. He would not let anyone else die alone.

Joe finished medical school. He was working as an **intern**. His work was overseen by a doctor. A man whom Joe took care of was dying. Joe looked for the man's family. The search took him to a homeless shelter. It was called Camillus House. Joe saw how little help the people there had for their health problems. He set up a free clinic there. That was in 1984.

But, Joe did not stay inside and wait for patients. He went to the streets. He looked under bridges, in alleys, and in parks. He found people without homes and told them about the clinic. He promised to help them.

At first, Joe had no help. He paid for supplies. He asked people to give furniture and medicine. He talked people into helping for free. The number of sick people who came for help kept growing.

Joe started to write to the government and charities for money. This money is called grant money. He was very good at talking people into helping him keep the clinic open. He was so good that he was able to open two more clinics. One was in a neighborhood called Little Havana in Miami, Florida. The other was near a camp for farm workers.

In 1991, Joe joined a task force. This group helped the government learn more about health care for the poor. That same year, he became the first person to teach about health care for the homeless at a medical school in Miami. Students at the school work at the free clinics so that they can learn more about helping the poor. Today, Joe's first tiny clinic is a big building with more than 250 workers. Two hundred of them give their time for free.

In 1993, Joe was given an important grant. It is known as a "genius grant." Its real name is a MacArthur Fellowship. It is money given to people who are creative and solve problems or do important work in the United States. Joe has done both. His help for the poor has changed the lives of many in Miami.

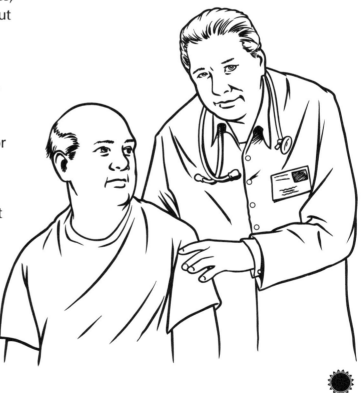

Hispanic American Achievers   © Carson-Dellosa • CD-104256

Pedro José "Joe" Greer
(1956– _____)

1. This passage tells about:

   a. a man who never got over the death of his sister.

   b. a doctor who made it his mission to help the poor.

   c. a doctor who runs a clinic for wealthy people.

   d. a man who became a doctor.

2. What does the word **intern** mean in the passage?

   a. someone who works for a company in a high-level job

   b. someone who cannot learn on the job and has to go back to school

   c. someone who just finished medical school and works under another doctor

   d. someone who has to learn another skill before he can finish school

3. Number the following events in the order they happened.

   _____ Joe was given a "genius grant."

   _____ Joe joined a task force to help advise the government.

   _____ Joe opened two more clinics.

   _____ Joe got money, medicine, and furniture for his first clinic.

   _____ Joe went to medical school.

4. Answer the following questions.

   What promise did Joe make to himself after his sister died?

   _____

   _____

   What was the name of the shelter where Joe started his first clinic?

   _____

   Where did Joe go to look for patients?

   _____

   _____

   What was Joe given in 1993?

   _____

5. What is another way of saying "Joe felt that he had failed her"?

   a. Joe felt that he had forgotten about her.

   b. Joe felt that he had let her down.

   c. Joe felt that he had flunked out.

   d. Joe felt that he had aided her.

Bonus

Have you ever done something to help others in your neighborhood or town? Write a paragraph about a charity you could help or a group for which your class could raise money.

Nancy Lopez
(1957– ____)

Nancy Lopez played golf with all of her heart and was always cheerful, a fact that made an enormous difference to her fans. When Nancy was 15 years old, she saw a professional golfer be **rude** to a fan by turning him away when he asked for an autograph. Nancy thought to herself that she would never act like that. Other golfers and her fans loved her for it.

Nancy started playing golf with her father when she was 8 years old and received a set of golf clubs as a gift. The next year, she won a children's tournament in New Mexico, her home state. When she was 12 years old, she won a state championship. Nancy made golf look easy, but it was not easy for Nancy to practice her sport. She is a Hispanic American. Because of that, she was not allowed to play at a nearby golf course. Instead, she and her parents had to drive 200 miles to a course where Hispanic Americans could play. It was a dry, dusty course with dead grass in many places, but it was the best course open to them.

Nancy also faced difficulties in golf because she is a woman. Some courses would not let women play until late in the day. In high school, there was no girls' golf team, so Nancy had to petition to join the boys' team instead. She helped them win the state championship.

Her father aided Nancy in many ways with her ambitions. He taught her what he knew about golf and gave her tips about the game. He dug a big pit in their backyard and filled it with sand so that Nancy could use it to learn how to hit balls out of sand traps.

When Nancy started to play professional golf, many people complained. They said that she was too focused on her game, and they did not like the way she played. The truth was that they did not like to see a Hispanic American woman win so many games. Nancy just ignored the prejudice like she always had. She concentrated and worked hard. In 1977, she played in six professional events. Her first full year as a professional golfer was 1978, and she won nine tournaments, including five tournaments in a row. No female golfer has ever beaten her record.

By the time Nancy was 30, she had won 35 tournaments. In 1989, she was added to the Ladies Professional Golf Association (LPGA) Hall of Fame, becoming the youngest woman to have that honor.

Nancy set a goal for herself. She wanted to win 50 tournaments before she retired, and she almost reached that goal. She retired from full-time play in 2002 after winning 48 times, because she knew that it was the right time to retire. She had injured her knees. She had three children and wanted to spend more time with her family. Nancy left golf, but golfers will never forget the amazing career of Nancy Lopez.

Nancy Lopez
(1957– _____)

Nancy Lopez played golf with all of her heart. She always seemed happy. It made a big difference to her fans. When Nancy was 15 years old, she saw a professional golfer be **rude** to a fan. Nancy thought to herself that she would never act like that. Other golfers and her fans loved her for it.

Nancy started playing golf with her father when she was 8 years old. She got a set of golf clubs as a gift. The next year, she won a children's tournament in New Mexico, her home state. When she was 12, she won a state championship! Nancy made golf look easy. But, it was not easy for Nancy to practice. She is a Hispanic American. Because of that, she was not allowed to play at a nearby golf course. Instead, she and her parents had to drive 200 miles to a course where they could play. It was a dry, dusty course. In many places, there was dead grass. But, it was the best course that was open to them.

Nancy also had problems in golf because she is a woman. Some courses would not let women play until late in the day. In high school, there was no girls' golf team. Nancy had to play on the boys' team. She helped them win the state championship.

Her father helped Nancy in many ways. He taught her what he knew about golf. He gave her tips about the game. He dug a big pit in their backyard. He filled it with sand. Nancy used this to learn how to hit balls out of sand traps.

When Nancy started to play professional golf, many people complained. They said that she was too focused on her game. They did not like the way she played. The truth was that they did not like to see a Hispanic American woman win so many games. Nancy ignored the prejudice like she always had. She kept working hard. In 1977, she played in six professional events. Her first full year as a professional golfer was 1978. She won nine tournaments. She also won five tournaments in a row. No female golfer has ever beaten her record.

By the time Nancy was 30, she had won 35 tournaments. In 1989, she was added to the Ladies Professional Golf Association (LPGA) Hall of Fame. She was the youngest woman to have that honor.

Nancy set a goal for herself. She wanted to win 50 tournaments before she retired. She almost reached that goal. She retired from full-time play in 2002. She had won 48 times. But, she knew that it was the right time to retire. Her knees were hurt. She had three children. She wanted to spend more time with her family. Nancy left golf, but golfers will never forget the amazing career of Nancy Lopez.

Hispanic American Achievers

Nancy Lopez
(1957– _____)

1. This passage tells about:

   a. a girl who wanted to play many sports.

   b. a girl whose parents did not like golf.

   c. a Hispanic American woman who overcame prejudice and became a great golfer.

   d. a woman who played golf in the southwestern United States but retired because she did not like the game.

2. What does the word **rude** mean in the passage?

   a. to act without good manners

   b. work done in a rough way, without skill

   c. to be in a natural state

   d. a wild, unsettled land

3. Number the following events in the order they happened.

   _____ Nancy decided to retire from golf.

   _____ Nancy was voted into the LPGA Hall of Fame.

   _____ Nancy helped her high school team win a state championship.

   _____ Nancy played her first full year as a professional golfer.

   _____ Nancy won a children's golf tournament in New Mexico.

4. Answer the following questions.

   In what year was Nancy Lopez born?

   _____

   What was one way that Nancy's father helped her play golf?

   _____

   _____

   In how many professional events did Nancy play in 1977?

   _____

   How many professional tournaments did Nancy win in her career?

   _____

5. Why did Nancy's parents drive 200 miles to let her play golf?

   a. They wanted their daughter to play at the best possible golf course.

   b. There were other courses closer to home, but Nancy and her parents were not allowed to use them.

   c. There were no golf courses close to their home.

   d. none of the above

Bonus

Have you ever seen a golf game on TV? Watch a game. How is it different from watching a baseball or football game? Write a paragraph that compares watching the two events.

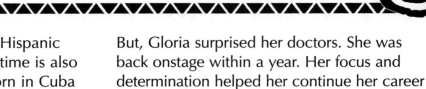

Gloria Estefan
(1957– _____)

One of the most popular Hispanic American singers of all time is also a **survivor**. Gloria Estefan was born in Cuba in 1957. That was a time when many Cubans were fighting against their leader, Fidel Castro.

Gloria and her family had to flee Cuba to the United States. With little money, they had to live in a very poor section of Miami, Florida. Gloria's mother had to get a job to support the family while Gloria went to school and took care of her ailing father.

At the age of 12, Gloria was given a guitar, and she taught herself how to play. Her future husband, Emilio, was impressed with Gloria's singing voice. He asked her to join his band. Gloria agreed to sing with his band but only on the weekends. She was determined to finish her college degree. That kind of focus would help her later in her life.

Gloria joined the band, called the Miami Sound Machine. The group recorded songs in Spanish and English. They had many hit songs. In 1986, they had a hit song called "Conga" that was number one on the pop, Latin, soul, and dance charts—all at the same time.

Gloria's amazing success continued until March 20, 1990. The band was traveling on a tour, and Gloria was napping in the backseat of their tour bus. Suddenly, a large semitruck hit the bus in the rear, where Gloria was sleeping. She woke up on the floor of the bus. Her back was broken.

Gloria had surgery to have two rods placed in her back. She also had 400 stitches and survived months of pain. She had physical therapy that was very difficult.

But, Gloria surprised her doctors. She was back onstage within a year. Her focus and determination helped her continue her career despite the tragic accident.

Today, Gloria and her husband own five Cuban-themed restaurants and two hotels. She has written two books for children. They are about Noelle, her pet bulldog. And, Gloria still makes music. She has won many awards. In one interview, she said, "Music has been one of the most beautiful things in my life and will always be a very big part of who I am and what I do."

Gloria Estefan
(1957– _____)

One of the most well-known Hispanic American singers ever is also a **survivor**. Gloria Estefan was born in Cuba in 1957. That was a time when many Cubans were fighting against their leader, Fidel Castro.

Gloria and her family had to flee Cuba. With little money, they moved to a very poor part of Miami, Florida. Gloria's mother got a job to support the family. Gloria went to school. She also helped take care of her sick father.

Gloria was given a guitar when she was 12 years old. She taught herself how to play. A few years later, she met her future husband, Emilio. He loved Gloria's singing voice. He asked her to join his band. Gloria said yes. But, she also said that she would play only on the weekends. She wanted to finish college. That kind of focus helped her later in her life.

The band was called the Miami Sound Machine. The group sang songs in Spanish and English. They had many hit songs. One of their songs, "Conga," was number one on many music charts.

Then, on March 20, 1990, the band was on a tour bus. Gloria was sleeping in the back of the bus. A large truck hit the bus. It struck where Gloria was sleeping. She woke up on the floor. Her back was broken.

Gloria had surgery. The doctors put two steel rods in her back. She had 400 stitches. She was in pain for months. She had to work hard after the accident to get better.

But, Gloria surprised her doctors. She was back onstage within a year. Nothing could stop her.

Today, Gloria and her husband own five restaurants and two hotels. She has written two books for children. They are about Noelle, her pet bulldog. And, Gloria still makes music. She has won many awards. In one interview, she said, "Music has been one of the most beautiful things in my life and will always be a very big part of who I am and what I do."

Gloria Estefan
(1957– _____)

1. What is the main idea of this passage?

   a. Gloria Estefan was in a bus accident.

   b. Gloria Estefan is a great singer who did not let an accident stop her career.

   c. Gloria Estefan took care of her sick father.

   d. Gloria Estefan is a great singer.

2. What does the word **survivor** mean in the passage?

   a. someone who suffers

   b. someone who forgets the past

   c. someone who lives through a hard or painful time

   d. someone who wins many awards

3. Number the following events in the order they happened.

   _____ Gloria went to school in Miami, Florida.

   _____ Gloria went back onstage after her surgery.

   _____ Gloria was born when many Cubans were fighting against their leader.

   _____ Gloria wrote two children's books.

   _____ Gloria joined a band.

4. Answer the following questions.

   Gloria sings songs in what two languages?

   _____

   What was the date of Gloria's accident in the tour bus?

   _____

   How old was Gloria when she got her first guitar?

   _____

   How long did it take Gloria to recover from her accident?

   _____

5. Who taught Gloria how to play the guitar?

   a. Her father taught her how to play the guitar.

   b. Her husband taught her how to play the guitar.

   c. She taught herself how to play the guitar.

   d. none of the above

Bonus

Do you know someone or have you read about someone who is a survivor? Write a paragraph about what the person survived or overcame and how he or she accomplished this.

Ellen Ochoa
(1958– _____)

When Ellen Ochoa was growing up, she did not dream about going into space. At that time, there were no female astronauts in America to act as **role models**. It was not until Ellen was 20 years old that Sally Ride and five other women were chosen for the space program. By that time, Ellen was in college. More than 10 years later, Ellen was working on her PhD, and a group of her friends applied for jobs at the National Aeronautics and Space Administration (NASA). They told Ellen, and she applied, too. It was Ellen who was selected by NASA. She became an astronaut in 1990.

Ellen grew up in La Mesa, California. Her mother loved to learn. She raised five children and went to college at the same time. She could take only one class at a time, so it took Ellen's mother 22 years to finish school. Her mother's hard work made Ellen want to work hard, too.

That was a good thing, because the training at NASA was difficult and demanding. Ellen had to learn how to cope with every kind of emergency that might occur. The hours were long and tiring. Ellen says that being in space was actually much easier than training to go there!

Ellen was the first Hispanic American woman to fly into space. Her first mission was in 1993, when she was in space for nine days. It was Ellen's job to launch a satellite, using the shuttle's mechanical arm. She also helped her team conduct research about the atmosphere. She stayed in touch with her family on Earth through e-mail, and on trips that are longer than 10 days, astronauts also get to see their families on video conference calls.

Since that first flight, Ellen has gone into space three more times. She has logged 978 hours in space and worked the mechanical arm on each trip. Ellen loves going into space. She finds it exciting and interesting.

Back on Earth, Ellen has other jobs to do. She worked as an inventor, and one of her inventions helps guide robot systems and make them work more efficiently. Ellen is now in charge of the Astronaut Office at NASA in Houston, Texas. Ellen enjoys going to schools and speaking to students. She wants to demonstrate that they can do anything they want to if they work hard and love learning. That is the same lesson that Ellen's mother taught her.

When Ellen is not working, she spends time with her family. She is married and has two children. She likes to play volleyball and ride her bike. Music is another hobby—Ellen plays the flute. But, her favorite hobby is flying. She pilots a small plane. Even when she cannot go into space, Ellen loves to be in the sky.

Ellen Ochoa
(1958– _____)

When Ellen Ochoa was growing up, she did not dream about going into space. At that time, there were no female astronauts in America to act as **role models**. It was not until Ellen was 20 years old that Sally Ride and five other women were picked for the space program. By that time, Ellen was in college. Ten years later, Ellen was working on her PhD. A group of her friends applied for jobs at the National Aeronautics and Space Administration (NASA). They told Ellen. She applied, too. And, Ellen was the person NASA picked. She became an astronaut in 1990.

Ellen grew up in La Mesa, California. Her mother loved to learn. She raised five children and went to college at the same time. She could take only one class at a time. So, it took Ellen's mother 22 years to finish school. Her mother's hard work made Ellen want to work hard, too.

That was a good thing. The training at NASA was hard work. Ellen had to learn how to deal with every kind of event that might go wrong. The hours were long and hard. Ellen says that being in space was much easier than training to go there!

Ellen was the first Hispanic American woman to fly into space. Her first mission was in 1993. She was in space for nine days. It was Ellen's job to launch a satellite. She used the shuttle's robot arm to do this. She also helped her team do research about the atmosphere. She stayed in touch with her family on Earth through e-mail. On trips that are longer than 10 days, astronauts also get to see their families on video calls.

Since that first flight, Ellen has gone into space three more times. She has spent 978 hours in space. On each trip, she worked the robot arm. Ellen loves going into space. She finds it exciting and interesting.

Back on Earth, Ellen has other jobs to do. She worked as an inventor. One of her inventions helps guide robot systems and make them work better. Ellen is now in charge of the Astronaut Office at NASA. She works in Houston, Texas. Ellen likes to go to schools and speak to students. She wants to show them that they can do anything they want to if they work hard and love to learn. That is the same lesson that Ellen's mother taught her.

When Ellen is not working, she spends time with her family. She is married and has two children. She likes to play volleyball. She also likes to ride her bike. Music is another hobby. Ellen plays the flute. But, her favorite hobby is flying. She pilots a small plane. Even when she cannot go into space, Ellen loves to be in the sky.

Ellen Ochoa
(1958– _____)

1. Which of the following words best describes Ellen Ochoa?

   a. dreamy

   b. hardworking

   c. silly

   d. quirky

2. What does the term **role models** mean in the passage?

   a. small models of human beings that show what the inside of the body looks like

   b. people we can look up to and learn from

   c. people who make bread and rolls for a living

   d. people who go into space

3. Number the following events in the order they happened.

   _____ Ellen grew up in La Mesa, California.

   _____ Ellen became an astronaut.

   _____ Ellen was put in charge of the Astronaut Office at NASA.

   _____ Ellen went on her first trip into space.

   _____ Ellen applied for a job at NASA for the first time.

4. Answer the following questions.

   How did Ellen find out about jobs at NASA?

   _____

   _____

   What kind of woman was Ellen's mother?

   _____

   _____

   How many hours has Ellen spent in space?

   _____

   When can astronauts see their families on video calls?

   _____

   _____

5. Which of the following is a list of Ellen's hobbies?

   a. biking, flying, and playing baseball

   b. flying, playing volleyball, and playing the flute

   c. playing volleyball, playing water polo, and skydiving

   d. flying, writing music, and blogging

Bonus

Think of an invention that could help people around the world. Write a story about it.

Alberto Salazar
(1958– _____)

It was a race that made history. Two young men pounded across 26.2 miles without one moment's pause. The year was 1982, the race was the Boston Marathon, and the two runners were Alberto Salazar and Dick Beardsley.

When the race began, all of the runners crowded across a narrow bridge in Hopkinton, Massachusetts. For a week, Alberto had been staying with his parents. His leg hurt and felt tight. It was an unusually warm day for the race, and other runners started to fall behind. But, Alberto and Dick ran side by side. They tore up and down hills, racing toward Boston, Massachusetts. Alberto knew that he had to save his strength, because at the end of the race, he would need to surge ahead to win. And, he managed to do it. Alberto won the race by only two seconds.

Alberto was born in Havana, Cuba. His father was a friend of Fidel Castro's until Castro took over Cuba. In 1960, Alberto's father saw that the revolution was not going as he had hoped that it would. He knew that he had to remove his family from Cuba. Alberto's father was an engineer, and he secured a good job near Boston.

Alberto and his brothers ran track in high school. Then, Alberto went to college in Oregon, where he won track awards and became a sports star at his school. Halfway through college, Alberto changed his goals and started to train for **marathons**. These long races take a special kind of training and discipline. Alberto was great in them from the start. He won the New York City Marathon three times in a row—in 1980, 1981, and 1982. After his huge 1982 win in Boston, he also captured American track wins in Sweden and Norway.

But, things were not all well. The hard struggle to win in Boston damaged Alberto's body. He was given a place on the 1984 Olympic team, but Alberto did not win any medals. He started to lose races, and eventually he could not even jog. It took him 10 years to gain back his health.

People thought that Alberto's running days were over, but he was tough. His toughness had helped him win long races, and it helped him get well. In 1994, he participated in a race in South Africa. It was a 53-mile route. Alberto amazed everyone by being the first runner to cross the finish line.

Alberto does not run in races any longer, but he still loves running. Now, he is a coach, helping young runners train for important events. And, Alberto's son carries on the family love of sports as a professional soccer player.

Alberto Salazar
(1958– ____)

It was a race that made history. Two young men ran 26.2 miles without one moment's pause. The year was 1982. The race was the Boston Marathon. And, the two runners were Alberto Salazar and Dick Beardsley.

When the race started, all of the runners crowded across a bridge in Hopkinton, Massachusetts. For a week, Alberto had stayed with his parents. His leg hurt and felt tight. It was a warm day. Other runners started to fall behind. But, Alberto and Dick ran side by side. They ran up and down hills. They ran toward Boston, Massachusetts. Alberto knew that he had to save his strength. At the end of the race, he would need to surge ahead to win. And, he did. Alberto won the race by only two seconds.

Alberto was born in Havana, Cuba. His father was a friend of Fidel Castro's. Then, Castro took over Cuba. In 1960, Alberto's father saw that things were not going well in Cuba. He knew that he had to take his family away. He got a good job near Boston.

Alberto and his brothers ran track in high school. Then, Alberto went to college in Oregon. He won track awards. But, he changed his goals. He started to train for **marathons**. These long races take a special kind of training. Alberto was great in them. He won the New York City Marathon three times in a row. He was the winner in 1980, 1981, and 1982. He won track events in Sweden and Norway in 1982, too.

But, things were not all well. The hard win in Boston hurt Alberto's body. Alberto was on the 1984 Olympic team. But, he did not win any medals. He started to lose races. Soon, he could not even jog. It took him 10 years to get back his health.

Everyone thought that Alberto's running days were over. But, Alberto was tough. His toughness had helped him win long races. It helped him get well. In 1994, he ran in a race in South Africa. It was 53 miles long. Alberto amazed everyone. He was the first runner to cross the finish line.

Alberto does not run in races anymore. But, he still loves running. Now, he is a coach. He helps young runners train for big events. And, Alberto's son carries on the family love of sports. He is a professional soccer player.

Alberto Salazar
(1958– _____)

1. What is the main idea of the last paragraph?

   a. Alberto and his family had to leave Cuba in 1960.

   b. Alberto works as a coach for runners today.

   c. Alberto won a race in South Africa.

   d. Alberto won the 1982 Boston Marathon at the last moment.

2. What does the word **marathons** mean in the passage?

   a. long races of 26.2 miles

   b. short races that need big surges at the end

   c. sports events in which athletes swim, bike, and run

   d. gymnastics events

3. Number the following events in the order they happened.

   _____ Alberto and his brothers were on the track team in high school.

   _____ Alberto won three New York City Marathons in a row.

   _____ Alberto started coaching young runners.

   _____ Alberto's family left Cuba.

   _____ Alberto went to college.

4. Answer the following questions.

   In what state did Alberto go to college?

   _____

   By how much time did Alberto win the 1982 Boston Marathon?

   _____

   How long was the race that Alberto ran in 1994?

   _____

   What kept Alberto from running between 1984 and 1994?

   _____

   _____

5. What happened to Alberto after the Boston Marathon?

   a. He had hurt his body, so he could not run for a long time.

   b. He did not like running and wanted to do something else for a living.

   c. He thought that he would go back to running track events.

   d. He won three medals at the Olympics in 1984.

Bonus

What is the hardest thing that you have ever done? Did you have to push your body or your mind? How did it turn out? Write a description of your achievement.

Evelyn Cisneros
(1959– _____)

The little girl was so shy that she did not want to sing. Evelyn Cisneros was four years old and in a children's choir. But, she was terrified of being onstage. While everyone sang, she started to lift up her dress. By the end of the song, she had pulled the dress over her head! She felt safe hidden inside its folds.

Evelyn grew up in California. Her grandparents were farm workers, and her parents wanted Evelyn and her brother to be proud of their Hispanic heritage. But, Evelyn's shyness got worse and worse. Finally, her mother made a plan to help fix the problem. She took Evelyn shopping one day, bought her ballet slippers, and enrolled her in a ballet class. At first, Evelyn hated it. On ballet class days, she pretended to be sick so that she did not have to go. Her mother firmly told her that she had to take the class for one year. By that time, Evelyn loved ballet.

Evelyn made time for dance even when it was difficult. Sometimes, she was on two or three sports teams at the same time that she was going to ballet classes. But, when she was 13 years old, Evelyn had to choose. She had only so much time. She chose dance because she could not imagine what her life would be like without ballet.

When Evelyn was only 15, she had a chance to dance professionally with the famous San Francisco Ballet. She decided to stay at home and complete school in Huntington Beach, California. She quickly finished high school. Then, she accepted a place in the ballet company. Evelyn was given a part three days after she arrived. Another dancer was hurt, leaving Evelyn with only five hours to learn the part.

Soon, Evelyn was one of the stars of the company. Special roles were created for her, and the public loved her. Evelyn was graceful and able to act and express emotions in the parts she danced. She **dazzled** the audiences who watched her.

Evelyn married another dancer from the ballet company in 1996 and retired in 1999. She was only 40 years old, but many dancers leave ballet when they are still young because ballet is so hard on the body. And, by that time, Evelyn had danced professionally for 23 years.

Evelyn feels that her life as a Hispanic American dancer has been significant. She wanted Hispanic children to see a dancer who looked like them. During her career, she danced in Mexico, Spain, and Cuba. Now, she teaches dance classes for Hispanic American children. She writes about ballet for *Dance Magazine*. Everything about dance, she says, fills her with joy.

The little girl was so shy that she did not want to sing. Evelyn Cisneros was four years old. She was in a choir. But, she was scared of being onstage. While everyone sang, she started to lift up her dress. By the end of the song, it was over her head! She felt safe hidden inside it.

Evelyn grew up in California. Her grandparents were farm workers. Her parents wanted Evelyn and her brother to be proud of their Hispanic background. But, Evelyn's shyness got worse and worse. It got so bad that her mother made a plan to help. She took Evelyn to a store one day. She bought her ballet slippers. She put her in a ballet class. At first, Evelyn hated it. She pretended to be sick so that she did not have to go to class. Her mother told her that she had to take the class for one year. By that time, Evelyn loved ballet.

Evelyn made time for ballet even when it was hard. Sometimes, she was on two or three sports teams at the same time that she was dancing. But, when she was 13 years old, Evelyn had to choose. She had only so much time. She chose dance. She could not think of what her life would be like without ballet.

Evelyn was only 15 when she had a chance to dance onstage. It was with the San Francisco Ballet. She chose to stay at home and finish school in Huntington Beach, California. She quickly finished high school. Then, she took a place in the well-known ballet company. Evelyn was given a part three days after she started. Another dancer was hurt. Evelyn had only five hours to learn the part.

Soon, Evelyn was one of the stars of the company. Special roles were created for her. The public loved her. Evelyn was graceful. She was able to act in the parts she danced. She **dazzled** the people who watched her.

Evelyn married another dancer from the ballet in 1996. She retired in 1999. She was only 40 years old. Many dancers leave ballet when they are young because it is so hard on the body. And, Evelyn had danced professionally for 23 years.

Evelyn feels that her life as a Hispanic American dancer has been important. She wanted Hispanic children to see a dancer who looked like them. During her career, she danced in Mexico, Spain, and Cuba. Now, she teaches dance classes for Hispanic American children. She writes about ballet for *Dance Magazine*. She says that everything about dance fills her with joy.

Evelyn Cisneros
(1959– _____)

1. The fourth paragraph of this passage is mostly about:

   a. how Evelyn started ballet classes.

   b. what Evelyn was like as a little girl.

   c. Evelyn's family in Huntington Beach, California.

   d. how Evelyn started dancing with the San Francisco Ballet.

2. What does the word **dazzled** mean in the passage?

   a. amazed or astonished with something wonderful

   b. slowly sprinkled with liquid

   c. went blind for a few moments

   d. felt things whirl around

3. Number the following events in the order they happened.

   _____ Evelyn started taking ballet classes.

   _____ Evelyn sang in a children's choir.

   _____ Evelyn danced with the San Francisco Ballet.

   _____ Evelyn gave up sports to spend all of her time on ballet.

   _____ Evelyn started writing for a magazine about dance.

4. Answer the following questions.

   What problem did Evelyn's mother want to fix with ballet classes?

   _____

   Why did Evelyn turn down her first offer from the San Francisco Ballet?

   _____

   _____

   How long did Evelyn have to learn her first part for the ballet company?

   _____

   What kind of classes does Evelyn teach?

   _____

5. Why do many ballet dancers retire when they are still young?

   a. Ballet is not very much fun.

   b. Ballet is hard on the body.

   c. Ballet is boring.

   d. Ballet is difficult to learn.

Bonus

Were you shy when you were younger? Do you know someone who is shy? Write a story about a shy person who finds a way to overcome his or her shyness.

Salma Hayek
(1966– ____)

Salma Hayek was born in Mexico to an opera singer mother and an oil executive father. They lived in a small town where Salma kept two deer for pets. Her family enjoyed skiing in Colorado during vacations.

Salma loved the United States and begged her parents to send her to school there. At last, she got her wish; she was enrolled in a Louisiana boarding school when she was 12 years old. But Salma, filled with mischief, loved to play practical jokes and tricks. After two years, the school had had enough and asked her to leave.

Salma chose to go to college in Mexico City, Mexico. To please her parents, she studied **political science** so that she could learn about world governments and international relations. But, she also secretly took acting classes. She got parts in college plays, where people working in TV saw her acting. They offered her a small part on a TV show. Then, in 1989, she got the lead role on a TV show called *Teresa*. Overnight, everyone in Mexico knew Salma's name. She became a big star there.

At that time, few movies were made in Mexico. Salma wanted to make movies. So, she moved to Los Angeles, California, in 1991, knowing that the move meant that she would have to start over. She did not care. She took only two suitcases with her, and she signed up for an acting class. Nobody could understand her English, but she would not give up.

Salma got a small movie part in 1993. Her English got better, and her parts in movies got better, too. She was offered a role in *Wild, Wild West* in 1999. This was one of the roles for which people started to remember Salma's work.

Salma has had some interesting roles. She has played a Mexican artist and a thief. Most of her work now is in the United States, but sometimes she goes back to Mexico to make films, too.

In 2006, Salma returned to TV work. She saw a television show in Columbia that she liked and decided to bring a version of the show to American television. The show, called *Ugly Betty*, was a hit from the start. Salma is the producer of *Ugly Betty*, and she has also acted on the show. It is one way that she helps people learn more about life as a Hispanic American.

Salma Hayek
(1966– ____)

Salma Hayek was born in Mexico. Her mother was an opera singer. Her father worked for an oil company. They lived in a small town. Salma kept two deer for pets. Her family went skiing in Colorado for vacations.

Salma loved the United States. She begged her parents to send her to school there. At last, she got to go to a boarding school when she was 12 years old. The school was in Louisiana. But, Salma loved to play jokes and tricks. After two years, the school had had enough. They asked her to leave.

Salma chose to go to college in Mexico City, Mexico. To please her parents, she studied **political science** to learn about world governments. But, she also took acting classes in secret. She got parts in college plays. Some people working in TV saw her in one play. They gave her a small part on a TV show. Then, in 1989, she got the lead role on a TV show called *Teresa*. Soon, everyone in Mexico knew who Salma was. She was a big star there.

At that time, few movies were made in Mexico. Salma wanted to make movies. So, she moved to Los Angeles, California. It was 1991. The move meant that she would have to start over. She did not care. She took only two suitcases with her. She took an acting class. Nobody could understand her English. But, she would not give up.

Salma got a small movie part in 1993. Her English got better. Her parts in movies got better, too. She got a part in *Wild, Wild West* in 1999. Many people saw the movie. Salma's role in this movie helped people start to remember her work.

Salma has had some interesting roles. She has played a Mexican artist. She has played a thief. Most of her work is in the United States. Sometimes, she goes back to Mexico to make films, too.

In 2006, Salma went back to TV work. She saw a TV show in Columbia that she liked. She wanted to bring the show to American television. The show is called *Ugly Betty*. It was a big hit from the start. Salma is the producer of the show. She has also acted on the show. It is one way that she helps people learn more about life as a Hispanic American.

Salma Hayek
(1966– ____)

1. The fourth paragraph of the passage is mostly about:

   a. Salma's childhood.

   b. how Salma went to school in the United States.

   c. how Salma got her first acting job on a TV show.

   d. why Salma moved to Los Angeles, California, after acting in Mexico.

2. What does the term **political science** mean in the passage?

   a. the study of biology in modern life

   b. the study of governments and politics

   c. the study of different groups of animals

   d. the study of history

3. Number the following events in the order they happened.

   _____ Salma kept two deer for pets.

   _____ Salma got her first part in an American movie.

   _____ Salma got a part in the movie *Wild, Wild West*.

   _____ Salma started producing a TV show called *Ugly Betty*.

   _____ Salma went to school in Louisiana.

4. Answer the following questions.

   Where did Salma go to school when she was 12 years old?

   _____

   What is one role that Salma has played in a movie?

   _____

   _____

   What did Salma's mother do for a living?

   _____

   What was the name of the popular TV show in which Salma played the lead?

   _____

5. Why was Salma willing to give up her fame in Mexico and start over in Los Angeles?

   a. She did not like Mexico, and she wanted a fresh start in a new country.

   b. She knew that there were not many movies being made in Mexico.

   c. She wanted to pursue a new career besides acting.

   d. all of the above

Bonus

Do you think that your parents want you to have a certain kind of job or career when you grow up? Do you want to do something different? Write a paragraph explaining how you feel about the job you would most like to do.

Rebecca Lobo
(1973– _____)

Rebecca Lobo grew up in Connecticut, but her grandfather came to the United States from Cuba. Rebecca's family loved sports. Her sister and brother played basketball often, and Rebecca joined them. She was five years old when she learned the rules of the game. She was in fourth grade when she went to her first basketball camp.

Rebecca's parents were both teachers. Rebecca started to play on a basketball team in fourth grade, but her grades dropped. Her mother immediately told Rebecca that she would have to quit basketball if her grades did not improve. Rebecca worked hard on her grades, and by the end of high school, she was second in her class. She studied hard because she could not bear to lose basketball. Sometimes, she worried about a test or came home in a bad mood. She would go outside to shoot baskets, and her worries would vanish. She got lost in the game.

Rebecca's parents did not stop her from playing basketball as long as she kept good grades. In fact, they helped her many times. When she was in fourth grade, for example, a teacher told her that she should stop playing basketball with the boys at recess and start wearing a dress to class. Rebecca's parents were outraged, and they told her not to believe what her teacher had said. Rebecca said that she understood at that moment that she could play her sport and do her best to win, just like people thought boys could.

And, that is what she did. Rebecca started college in 1991, played sports, and studied hard. In 1993, her mother became ill with cancer. Rebecca spent as much time as she could with her mother. In 1996, Rebecca and her mother wrote a book called *The Home Team,* about their cancer experience.

In 1994, Rebecca's college team, the Connecticut Huskies, had an incredible, undefeated season and won the National Collegiate Athletic Association (NCAA) title. It was Rebecca's personal high point in sports. In 1996, Rebecca finished her amazing college career in sports and became the youngest member of the 1996 Olympic basketball team. She won a gold medal.

The Women's National Basketball Association (WNBA) was just starting in 1996. Rebecca got a place on the New York Liberty team. She was the only Hispanic American player. In 2002, she hurt her knee and was traded to the Houston Comets.

Rebecca retired from professional sports in 2003. Her knee problems made her leave the court earlier than she would have liked. But, she is still in the game—she does sports commentary about basketball on TV and coaches young basketball players. She also raises money to help people with cancer. She still makes a mark on the world with her winning **attitude**.

Rebecca Lobo
(1973– _____)

Rebecca Lobo grew up in Connecticut. Her grandfather came to the United States from Cuba. Rebecca's family loved sports. Her sister and brother played basketball a lot. Rebecca joined them. She was five years old when she learned how to play the game. She was in fourth grade when she went to her first basketball camp.

Rebecca's parents were both teachers. Rebecca started to play on a basketball team in fourth grade. Her grades started to drop. Her mother told Rebecca that she would have to quit basketball if her grades did not get better. Rebecca worked hard on her grades. She was second in her class by the end of high school. She loved basketball too much to lose it. Sometimes, she worried about a test. Sometimes, she was in a bad mood. She would go outside to shoot baskets. It always helped. She got lost in the game.

Rebecca's parents did not stop her from playing basketball if she kept good grades. In fact, they helped her many times. Once, when she was in fourth grade, a teacher told her that she should stop playing basketball with the boys at recess. The teacher said that Rebecca should start wearing a dress to class. Rebecca's parents were angry. They told her not to believe what her teacher had said. Rebecca said that she knew then that she could play her sport. She could do her best to win, just like people thought boys could.

And, that is what she did. Rebecca started college in 1991. She played sports and studied hard. In 1993, her mother got cancer. Rebecca spent as much time as she could with her mother. In 1996, Rebecca and her mother wrote a book about their experience with cancer. It is called *The Home Team*.

In 1994, Rebecca's college team, the Connecticut Huskies, had an undefeated season. They won the National Collegiate Athletic Association (NCAA) title. It is Rebecca's favorite moment in her career. In 1996, Rebecca finished her amazing college career in sports. She got a place as the youngest member on the 1996 Olympic basketball team. She won a gold medal.

The Women's National Basketball Association (WNBA) was just starting in 1996. Rebecca got a place on the New York Liberty team. She was the only Hispanic American player. In 2002, she hurt her knee and was traded to the Houston Comets.

Rebecca retired from professional sports in 2003. Her knee problems made her leave the court earlier than she would have liked. But, she is still in the game—she talks about basketball on TV. She coaches young basketball players. She also raises money to help people with cancer. She still makes a mark on the world with her winning **attitude**.

Rebecca Lobo
(1973– _____)

1. What is the main idea of the second paragraph?

    a. Rebecca's parents wanted her to work on her grades ahead of sports.

    b. Rebecca's parents would not let her teacher upset her.

    c. Rebecca's parents taught her how to play basketball.

    d. Rebecca's parents both became ill with cancer in the 1990s.

2. What does the word **attitude** mean in the passage?

    a. to attract other people's attention

    b. to tune into something

    c. a bad personality

    d. a feeling or a state of mind

3. Number the following events in the order they happened.

    _____ Rebecca learned the rules of basketball and played with her sister and brother.

    _____ Rebecca was traded to the Houston Comets.

    _____ Rebecca's grandfather came to the United States from Cuba.

    _____ Rebecca retired from professional basketball and works on TV.

    _____ Rebecca's college team had an undefeated season.

4. Answer the following questions.

    What was the Olympic team (year and sport) on which Rebecca played?

    _____

    What is the title of the book that Rebecca and her mother wrote?

    _____

    What is the name of the first professional team for which Rebecca played?

    _____

    Who told Rebecca to stop playing basketball and start wearing dresses?

    _____

5. What does it mean to "make your mark on the world"?

    a. to paint something on a wall or bridge

    b. to have a lasting effect on others through something you do

    c. to have a lot of money

    d. to know how to write your name

Bonus

Rebecca's favorite sports memory is when her college team won a championship. What is your favorite memory of your life? Write a story about it.

Mary Rodas
(1977– _____)

Mary Rodas was born on Christmas Day. Maybe that was a sign that the little girl would adore toys. Her love of playthings—and her creative ingenuity—led her to an amazing path of early success.

Mary's father came to New York City from El Salvador. He was the supervisor of a big apartment building. One day, Mary went with her father to the building and watched a man who lived there lay tiles. She told the man exactly why he was putting down the tiles in the wrong directions. She was four years old.

The man was Donald Spector, an inventor and the owner of a toy company. He was deeply impressed by Mary's strong-mindedness and good advice. He had many toys in his apartment that were new designs for his company. He asked Mary what she thought about them. She played with the toys and told Don her impressions. She gave him creative ideas for how to change the toys to improve them and make them more appealing.

By the time Mary was 14 years old, she had aided Don in his design work for 10 years. He had another new toy for her to examine. It was a balloon ball. The balloon ball was inside a cloth cover. Kids could add water to make it into a sports ball, popcorn to make it noisy and fun, or pennies to make it zigzag when they threw it. But, kids did not like it.

Mary knew why. The ball was orange, and it did not look inviting and fun. She picked out crazy, bright colors for the cloth. Suddenly, everyone clamored to buy one of the balls. It made millions of dollars for the company.

Don made Mary his vice president, even though she was only 14 years old. She was the youngest business executive in the country.

Mary had a lot of ideas for interesting new toys. She had the idea of a water squirter hidden inside a hand puppet. She also created a magic kit with a video that showed exactly how to do each trick. Kids did not have to ask their parents to help them read the instructions.

During college, Mary kept working for the toy company. She made a lot of people happy with her **clever** ideas. But, after she graduated, she decided to do something new in her career. Now, Mary works at a school herself—a school in New York City that combines medical ideas from around the world. Mary is in charge of choosing people to study at the school. She loves to talk to each person and take the time to learn about him—just like Don did with her years ago.

Hispanic American Achievers

Mary Rodas
(1977– _____)

Mary Rodas was born on Christmas Day. Maybe that was a sign that the little girl would love toys. Her love of toys—and her creative ideas—led her to an amazing life.

Mary's father came to New York City from El Salvador. He took care of a big apartment building. One day, Mary went with him. She was four years old. One of the people who lived there was laying tiles. Mary watched him. Then, she told him why he was putting down the tiles in the wrong way.

The man was Donald Spector. He owned a toy company. He was impressed by Mary. She was strong-minded. She gave him good advice. He had many toys in his apartment. They were new. He asked Mary what she thought about them. She played with them. She told Don what she thought. She gave him ideas for how to change the toys to make them better.

By the time Mary was 14 years old, she had helped Don for 10 years. He had another new toy. It was a balloon ball. The balloon ball was inside a cloth cover. Kids could add water to make it into a sports ball. They could add popcorn to make it noisy and fun. They could add pennies to make it zigzag when they threw it. But, kids did not like it.

Mary knew why. The ball was orange. It did not look fun. She picked out crazy, bright colors for the cloth. Suddenly, everyone wanted the ball. It made millions of dollars for the toy company.

Don made Mary his vice president. She was only 14 years old. She was the youngest business executive in the country.

Mary had a lot of ideas for great toys. She had the idea of a water squirter that was hidden inside a puppet. She also created a magic kit with a video that showed exactly how to do each trick. That meant kids did not have to ask their parents to help them.

During college, Mary kept working for the toy company. She made a lot of people happy with her **clever** ideas. But, after she graduated, she chose to do something new. Now, Mary works at a school. It is a school that combines health ideas from around the world. Mary is in charge of choosing people to study at the school. She loves to talk to each person and learn about him—just like Don did with her years ago.

Mary Rodas
(1977– _____)

1. Which of the following words best describes Mary Rodas?

   a. childish

   b. intelligent

   c. scared

   d. struggling

2. What does the word **clever** mean in the passage?

   a. smart and original

   b. calm and slow

   c. careful and complicated

   d. fast and uncontrolled

3. Number the following events in the order they happened.

   _____ Mary became a vice president at the age of 14.

   _____ Mary finished college.

   _____ Mary started working for a medical school.

   _____ Mary told Don Spector how to fix the tile he was laying.

   _____ Mary had an idea to improve the balloon ball.

4. Answer the following questions.

   How old was Mary when she met Don Spector?

   _____

   How did Mary make the balloon ball a big seller?

   _____

   _____

   What business did Mary work for during school?

   _____

   _____

   What country did Mary's father come from?

   _____

5. Why was Don Spector so impressed with Mary?

   a. She was strong-minded and smart.

   b. She could tell him what was right or wrong about a toy design.

   c. She gave him good advice when she was very young.

   d. all of the above

Bonus

If you could pick any business in the world to run, what would it be? What would you like to make? Write a paragraph telling about your choice.

Answer Key

Father Junípero Serra 7

1. a; 2. c; 3. 3, 2, 4, 5, 1;
4. It allowed him to use his mind and protected his health; He took a ship from Vera Cruz and walked to Mexico City, Mexico, from there; He was put in charge of the missions there; He had asthma and a hurt leg; 5. b

María Gertrudis de la Garza Falcón.....................10

1. b; 2. c; 3. 3, 2, 5, 4, 1; 4. She moved to Texas in 1750; He started a settlement on the Rio Grande River; The ranches had to be built like forts. Or, Spanish soldiers had to camp right on the ranch to keep people safe; She stayed in Texas and ran their huge ranch by herself; 5. a

David Glasgow Farragut.......13

1. d; 2. a; 3. 3, 5, 1, 2, 4; 4. David Porter was a navy captain who took care of David and who helped David find his first place on a ship; He had to capture the city of New Orleans, Louisiana; His ship was hit by cannon fire 240 times; David was given the rank of admiral; 5. b

Loreta Janeta Velasquez.......16

1. c; 2. d; 3. 1, 2, 5, 4, 3; 4. She said that she almost shot General Ulysses S. Grant; She dressed like a man so that she could go to war with her husband; The first battle in which Loreta fought was the First Battle of Bull Run; Loreta was wounded for the second time in the battle of Shiloh; 5. d

Adina De Zavala 19

1. c; 2. a; 3. 3, 1, 4, 5, 2; 4. The Alamo is an old Spanish mission that was used as a fort during a battle in 1836; The subject of her book was the Alamo; The markers show where historical events took place in Texas; "Hold the fort" means to protect a place; 5. c

Jovita Idar 22

1. b; 2. c; 3. 1, 5, 2, 4, 3; 4. *La Crónica* was a Spanish-language newspaper that Jovita's father started and that Jovita helped run; When the Rangers came to destroy her presses, Jovita blocked the doorway; Mexicans crossed into Texas to get away from the war in Mexico; *La Cruz Blanca* was a nursing group that Jovita started during the war. Or, The First Mexican Congress was a group that Jovita started during the war; 5. d

Marcelino Serna.................25

1. d; 2. d; 3. 4, 2, 3, 5, 1;
4. Marcelino was born in Mexico; He did not have to fight because he was not a U.S. citizen; Marcelino's company was sent to fight in France; France, Italy, England, and the United States gave Marcelino medals; 5. d

David Bennes Barkley..........28

1. b; 2. c; 3. 2, 4, 3, 1, 5; 4. David was born in Laredo, Texas; David feared that he would not be allowed to fight; He had to count the soldiers. Or, He had to find out where their guns were placed. Or, He needed to find out where the troops were located; General John J. Pershing, the man in charge of the American soldiers in WWI, praised David's brave act; 5. d

José Vicente Ferrer de Otero y Cintrón 31

1. c; 2. b; 3. 2, 3, 5, 4, 1; 4. José wanted to study at Princeton University; He acted in his first play the year after he finished college; José sang in *Man of La Mancha*; José directed movies. Or, José directed plays. Or, José sang and played the piano; 5. a

Francisca Flores.................34

1. b; 2. b; 3. 4, 5, 1, 2, 3; 4. Sleepy Lagoon was a place where young people went to swim; She helped get facts printed in the newspapers and aired on the radio; She was born in San Diego, California; She admired Dr. Martin Luther King Jr.'s work; 5. d

Romana Acosta Banuelos.....37

1. c; 2. c; 3. 4, 1, 3, 5, 2; 4. Romana named her business, Ramona Mexican Food Products, after her daughter; Romana saved money to buy a machine that made tortillas; The Pan American Bank gives minorities loans to buy houses and start businesses; Romana's daughter, Ramona, helps her run the bank; 5. d

César Estrada Chávez 40

1. a; 2. c; 3. 2, 4, 3, 5, 1; 4. César was not allowed to speak Spanish and did not know much English; The UFW is the union that César started to help farm workers; César lived on a small farm in Arizona; César was given the Medal of Freedom; 5. d

Lauro Cavazos 43

1. a; 2. b; 3. 5, 4, 3, 2, 1; 4. *Los Kineños* are the cowboys who work on the King Ranch; Lauro was made the president of the university; President Ronald Reagan asked Lauro to be the secretary of education; Lauro's family has lived in Texas for nearly 200 years; 5. b

Richard Alonso "Pancho" González............................46

1. c; 2. c; 3. 2, 1, 4, 5, 3; 4. His mother gave him his first tennis racket; He won a championship in Australia in 1954; The longest tennis match in history lasted 5 hours and 12 minutes; In 1955, Pancho made $15,000 and a white player made $80,000. Or, People said that Pancho's scar came from a knife fight; 5. c

Jaime Escalante 49

1. c; 2. a; 3. 2, 4, 1, 5, 3; 4. He did not have papers that would let him teach in California, and he did not speak English; The movie was called *Stand and Deliver*; Jaime taught math (calculus); The TV show showed students how to use their studies to find many kinds of jobs; 5. d

Rita Moreno 52

1. c; 2. a; 3. 2, 3, 4, 1, 5; 4. The Tony® Award is for work in stage plays; Rita was born in Puerto Rico; Rita wanted her daughter and other children to see a Puerto Rican in a TV show; They feel inspired because she showed them what is possible, regardless of race; 5. d

Cruz Reynoso 55

1. b; 2. c; 3. 1, 3, 4, 5, 2; 4. Cruz could not start school until the farm work was done for the year; President Bill Clinton honored Cruz's work; Cruz became a judge in 1976; Cruz studies and teaches about law. Or, Cruz studies and teaches about civil rights; 5. a

Roberto Clemente 58

1. b; 2. c; 3. 3, 1, 5, 2, 4; 4. The Brooklyn Dodgers was the first U.S. team to draft Roberto; Roberto played in the World Series in 1960 and 1971; In 1972, there was a big earthquake in Nicaragua; Roberto won the Gold Glove award for fielding 12 times; 5. a

Richard Serra 61

1. c; 2. d; 3. 3, 1, 2, 5, 4; 4. Richard's mother thought that thinking and doing interesting things were more important than material things; *Tilted Arc* was Richard's sculpture that was cut apart and taken down in New York City; Richard learned to work with steel in the steel mill where he worked during college; Richard's father worked in a jelly bean factory; 5. a

Miguel Algarin 64

1. b; 2. b; 3. 2, 4, 1, 3, 5; 4. Miguel was born in Puerto Rico; William Shakespeare inspired Miguel to tell stories; Miguel started asking artists and poets to come to his apartment in 1973; Poets and writers read their work there. Or, Artists show their work there. Or, People put on plays there. Or, Bands play music there; 5. a

Ritchie Valens 67

1. d; 2. d; 3. 1, 2, 5, 3, 4; 4. Bob Keane was a record producer who asked Ritchie to make his first record; Ritchie was 16 years old when he started to play in a band; Ritchie wrote about a girl whom he liked named Donna; Ritchie sang "La Bamba" in Spanish; 5. c

Pat Mora 70

1. a; 2. a; 3. 2, 3, 1, 4, 5; 4. Pat says that poets are healers because they find ways to build bridges between people; Pat started writing when she was about 40 years old; Doña Flor is a character in a tall tale that Pat wrote; Pat was given a typewriter when she finished eighth grade; 5. c

Isabel Allende 73

1. b; 2. d; 3. 1, 4, 3, 2, 5; 4. Isabel started to write a letter to her grandfather, and it turned into a novel; Isaisabel lived in the Middle East. Or, Isabel lived in Chile; Isabel's uncle was the president of Chile; Isabel wrote her first children's book in 2002; 5. a

Antonia Novello 76

1. b; 2. b; 3. 1, 2, 3, 5, 4; 4. Antonia's home country was Puerto Rico; Antonia's mother made sure that Antonia had the best teachers and opportunities, and she made her work hard even when she was not feeling well; President George H. W. Bush wanted Antonia to be the surgeon general; Antonia wanted all children be able to get shots. Or, Antonia wanted children to understand why they should not smoke; 5. b

Judy Baca 79

1. b; 2. c; 3. 1, 5, 2, 3, 4; 4. Judy learned about art history in college; More than 700 people helped Judy paint *The Great Wall of Los Angeles*; *The Great Wall of Los Angeles* tells how people of all races built the state of California together; Judy's mother used to draw pictures of Judy when she was a child; 5. b

Bill Richardson................... 82

1. c; 2. c; 3. 3, 5, 4, 1, 2; 4. Bill grew up in Mexico City, Mexico; Bill was sent to Boston, Massachusetts, to go to school; Bill became governor of New Mexico in 2002; President Bill Clinton asked Bill to be the secretary of energy; 5. a

France Anne Córdova.......... 85

1. a; 2. c; 3. 4, 5, 2, 1, 3; 4. *Apollo 11* was the first space mission in which men landed on the moon; France had 11 brothers and sisters; Pulsars are small pieces of a star that stay in space and glow after the star explodes; France thinks that we may find signs of life on Mars. Or, on Titan, a moon of Saturn. Or, on Europa, a satellite of Jupiter; 5. d

Answer Key

Horacio Gutiérrez.............88

1. b; 2. b; 3. 4, 5, 1, 3, 2;
4. Horacio and his family ran away from Fidel Castro's Cuba because it was dangerous; Juilliard is the best-known music school in the United States; George Perle is a composer who has written music just for Horacio to play; Horacio's mother was his first piano teacher; 5. d

Sonia Manzano 91

1. a; 2. c; 3. 1, 4, 2, 5, 3; 4. *No Dogs Allowed* is about a big family that takes a trip to the beach; Maria is the character whom Sonia plays on *Sesame Street*; Sonia acts on *Sesame Street* and also writes for the show; Today, Sonia acts on *Sesame Street*. Or, writes books. Or, gives speeches. Or, works for groups for children. Or, acts on Broadway; 5. c

Ileana Ros-Lehtinen............94

1. b; 2. d; 3. 1, 2, 5, 3, 4; 4. When Ileana was a state senator, she met her husband; She has voted to keep drilling away from the Florida coast and for money to help save sea animals and coral reefs; Ileana was 30 years old when she won her first election; Ileana wants low-cost loans for students because she feels that education is important; 5. d

Gary Soto 97

1. d; 2. a; 3. 1, 5, 3, 4, 2; 4. Gary knew that he wanted to write when he read poetry in college; Gary wrote his first children's book in 1987; Gary grew up in Fresno, California, so the city and the people who live there appear in many of Gary's poems and books; Gary feels that reading builds a life inside the mind; 5. b

Pedro José "Joe" Greer.......100

1. b; 2. c; 3. 5, 4, 3, 2, 1; 4. Joe promised that he would never let anyone else die alone; Joe started his first clinic at Camillus House; Joe looked for patients under bridges, in alleys, and in parks; Joe was given a MacArthur Fellowship, or a "genius grant"; 5. b

Nancy Lopez....................103

1. c; 2. a; 3. 5, 4, 2, 3, 1; 4. Nancy was born in 1957; Nancy's father drove her to a golf course where she could play. Or, Nancy's father built a sand trap in their backyard. Or, Nancy's father gave her tips about golf. Or, Nancy's father bought her a set of golf clubs; In 1977, Nancy played in six professional events; Nancy won 48 professional tournaments during her career; 5. b

Gloria Estefan 106

1. b; 2. c; 3. 2, 4, 1, 5, 3; 4. Gloria sings songs in English and Spanish; Gloria's bus accident happened on March 20, 1990; Gloria was 12 years old when she got her first guitar; It took Gloria about a year to recover from her accident; 5. c

Ellen Ochoa.....................109

1. b; 2. b; 3. 1, 3, 5, 4, 2; 4. Ellen's friends told her about the jobs at NASA; Ellen's mother was strong and hardworking; Ellen has spent 978 hours in space; Astronauts can see their families on video calls on trips that last more than 10 days; 5. b

Alberto Salazar 112

1. b; 2. a; 3. 2, 4, 5, 1, 3; 4. Alberto went to college in Oregon; Alberto won the 1982 Boston Marathon by two seconds; The race that Alberto ran in 1994 was 53 miles long; Alberto could not run between 1984 and 1994 because of poor health; 5. a

Evelyn Cisneros.................115

1. d; 2. a; 3. 2, 1, 4, 3, 5; 4. Evelyn's mother wanted to help Evelyn overcome her shyness with ballet classes; Evelyn turned down her first offer because she wanted to finish high school; Evelyn had five hours to learn her first part; Evelyn teaches dance classes for Hispanic American children; 5. b

Salma Hayek 118

1. d; 2. b; 3. 1, 3, 4, 5, 2; 4. Salma went to a boarding school in Louisiana; Salma has played a Mexican artist. Or, a thief; Salma's mother was an opera singer; The name of the TV show was *Teresa*; 5. b

Rebecca Lobo 121

1. a; 2. d; 3. 2, 4, 1, 5, 3; 4. Rebecca was on the 1996 Olympic team for women's basketball; The title of the book is *The Home Team*; Rebecca played for the New York Liberty team; A teacher told her to stop playing basketball and start wearing dresses when she was in fourth grade; 5. b

Mary Rodas 124

1. b; 2. a; 3. 3, 4, 5, 1, 2; 4. Mary was four years old when she met Don Spector; Mary made the balloon ball a big seller by adding more colors to the cloth cover; Mary worked for Don Spector's toy company during school; Mary's father came from El Salvador; 5. d

Assessment Grid

	MAIN IDEA (Question 1)	CONTEXT CLUES (Question 2)	SEQUENTIAL ORDER (Question 3)	READING FOR DETAILS (Question 4)	DRAWING CONCLUSIONS (Question 5)
Father Junípero Serra					
María Gertrudis de la Garza Falcón					
David Glasgow Farragut					
Loreta Janeta Velasquez					
Adina De Zavala					
Jovita Idar					
Marcelino Serna					
David Bennes Barkley					
José Vicente Ferrer de Otero y Cintrón					
Francisca Flores					
Romana Acosta Banuelos					
César Estrada Chávez					
Lauro Cavazos					
Richard Alonso "Pancho" González					
Jaime Escalante					
Rita Moreno					
Cruz Reynoso					
Roberto Clemente					
Richard Serra					
Miguel Algarin					
Ritchie Valens					
Pat Mora					
Isabel Allende					
Antonia Novello					
Judy Baca					
Bill Richardson					
France Anne Córdova					
Horacio Gutiérrez					
Sonia Manzano					
Ileana Ros-Lehtinen					
Gary Soto					
Pedro José "Joe" Greer					
Nancy Lopez					
Gloria Estefan					
Ellen Ochoa					
Alberto Salazar					
Evelyn Cisneros					
Salma Hayek					
Rebecca Lobo					
Mary Rodas					